VOICES OF CONVERGENCE

Voices of Convergence is one of the IMPACT BOOKS, a series designed to bring the modern reader the significant achievements of scholars, both Catholic and non-Catholic, in the fields of Scripture, Theology, Philosophy, Mathematics, History, and the Physical and Social Sciences. Among the titles in the series are:

This Good News: An Introduction to the Catholic Theology of the New Testament by Quentin Quesnell, S.J.
Maturing in Christ: St. Paul's Program for Growth in Christ by George Montague, S.M.
New Testament Essays by Raymond E. Brown, S.S.
Catechetics by Alfred McBride, O.Praem.
The God of Exodus by James Plastaras, C.M.
The Gospel of Eternal Life by Dominic M. Crossan, O.S.M.
The Word Dwells Among Us by William E. Lynch, C.M.
Jesus in the Synoptic Gospels by William E. Lynch, C.M.
The Person and the Group by John Thornhill, S.M.
Christ and Original Sin by Rev. Peter De Rosa
God Our Savior by Rev. Peter De Rosa
The Biblical Meaning of Man by Dom Wulstan Mork, O.S.B.
An Existential Approach to Theology by G. M. A. Jansen, O.P.
Jesus God and Man by Raymond E. Brown, S.S.
The Biblical Theology of the Secular by George Montague, S.M.
The Sacramental We by G. M. A. Jansen, O.P.
The Changing Face of Theology by Patrick Fannon, S.M.M.

VOICES OF CONVERGENCE

DANIEL J. LEARY

THE BRUCE PUBLISHING COMPANY / Milwaukee

Library of Congress Catalog Card Number: 68–55281

Copyright © 1969 The Bruce Publishing Company

TO VIRGINIA KENDALL

HELEN CHAN

SYLVIA LUTNES

ALL FOR DIFFERING

BUT CONVERGING REASONS

Acknowledgments

We are grateful to the following for permission to reprint copyrighted material:

The American Scholar, for citations from Buckminster Fuller's "Vision 65 Summary Lecture" (Spring, 1966) and from Marshall McLuhan's "Address at Vision 65" (Spring, 1966);

The Beacon Press, Boston, for citations from Herbert Marcuse's *Eros and Civilization*, Copyright © 1955, © 1966 by The Beacon Press;

Dr. Buckminster Fuller and The Saturday Review, Inc., for citations from Dr. Fuller's article "Man With a Chronofile," from *The Saturday Review* (April 1, 1967), Copyright © 1967 by The Saturday Review.

Dodd, Mead, and Company, New York, and The Society of Authors, London, for citations from George Bernard Shaw's *Complete Plays With Prefaces*, Copyright © 1963 by Dodd, Mead, and Company;

Harper & Row, Inc., New York, and Wm. Collins Sons & Co., Ltd., London for citations from Pierre Teilhard de Chardin's *The Phenomenon of Man*, Copyright © 1955 by Editions du Seuil, Paris; Copyright © 1959 in the English translation by W. Collins Sons & Co., Ltd., London, and Harper & Brothers, New York and for citations from Pierre Teilhard de Chardin's *The Divine Milieu*, Copyright © 1960 in the English translation by Wm. Collins Sons & Co., Ltd., London, and Harper & Brothers, Inc., New York;

Harper & Row, Inc., New York, for citations from Aldous Huxley's *Tomorrow and Tomorrow and Tomorrow*, Copyright © 1956 by Harper & Brothers, New York;

Herder & Herder, Inc., New York, for citations from Leslie Dewart's *The Future of Belief*, Copyright © 1966 by Herder & Herder;

J. B. Lippincott Company, Philadelphia, for citations from "To a Child," from *Hide and Seek* by Christopher Morley, Copyright 1920 by George H. Doran Co., copyright renewed 1948 by Christopher Morley;

McGraw-Hill Book Publishing Company, Inc., New York, for citations from Marshall McLuhan's *Understanding Media*, Copyright © 1964 by Marshall McLuhan;

The Macmillan Company, New York, for citations from Harvey Cox's *The Secular City*, Copyright © 1965 by The Macmillan Company, and for citations from Dietrich Bonhoeffer's *Letters and Papers From Prison*, Copyright © 1953 by The Macmillan Company;

The New Yorker Magazine, Inc., New York, for citations from Calvin Tomkins' article, "In the Outlaw Area" (January 8, 1966), Copyright © 1966 by The New Yorker;

Random House Inc., Pantheon Books, New York, for citations from Alan W. Watts' *The Joyous Cosmology*, Copyright © 1962 by Pantheon Books, Inc., and from Alan W. Watts' *Nature, Man and Woman*, Copyright © 1958 by Pantheon Books, Inc.;

Random House, Inc., New York, for citations from David T. Bazelon's *The Paper Economy*, Copyright © 1963 by Random House, Inc., from Norman O. Brown's *Love's Body*, Copyright © 1966 by Random House, Inc., from W. H. Auden's "Friday's Child" in *Homage to Clio*, Copyright © 1960 by Random House, Inc.;

Charles Scribners' Sons, New York, for citations from Martin Buber's *I and Thou*, Copyright © 1958 by Charles Scribners' Sons;

The Southern Illinois University Press, for citations from Buckminster Fuller's *No More Secondhand God*, Copyright © 1963 by Southern Illinois University Press.

Preface

The seed for this book was planted a good many years ago. I was taking a modern drama course and read with real anticipation an article by Father William Lynch in *Thought* on "Confusion in Our Theater." Already I recognized him to be a stimulating, probing commentator on the modern arts, in themselves and as reflectors of the spiritual and psychological health of society. My admiration has grown for Father Lynch with each of his books, but that particular article irritated me at the time and still does. In essence, he attempted to present the loss of tragic vision in modern drama as something rooted in the

> . . . twin heresies of Manichaeanism and Pelagianism. . . . The strain that runs through it all is obvious; it is the strain of dignity, strain of greatness, strain of exaltation, of transformation, of joy through pain, of the emergence of godlike qualities, of nobility.
>
> The great instigators of that realistic and naturalistic drama of the last century [viewed] the social environment as the great enemy, corrupted and corrupting, thoughtless, small, machinelike, contemptible, and in every case the origin of the tragic fact. . . . And this is what I mean by Manichaeanism.
>
> But there were compensations and they have been inevitable. These compensations were by way of discovering new, extraordinary and incalculable energies in man. The tragic dignity and magnitude begins to reside almost entirely in himself and in his reaction to such an environment, social or cosmic. He is never quite defeated and, if he is, he is going to squeeze something out of defeat for all it is worth. On such suppositions as the above, of course, such squeezing became absolutely essential because if we cannot twist the straight evidence of the Greeks for helplessness into exaltation then we are damned, really damned. It was an outburst of a unique Pelagianism, of such a kind as was never seen on land or sea.[1]

A few months after reading this article I saw Charles Laughton, Cedric Hardwick, Agnes Moorhead, and Charles

---

[1] William F. Lynch, S.J., "Confusion in Our Theater," *Thought* (Spring, 1951), pp. 343, 346.

Boyer in Shaw's "Don Juan in Hell Interlude." If this was
a product of the two-headed heresy, then I could only pray
that drama might continue to be so brilliantly delivered from
the orthodox. Chapter I of this book, which deals with Shaw
and Teilhard, is a direct result of that experience. In that
chapter, the most difficult in this book, I use the terms
Manichaeanism and Pelagianism to "twist" exaltation out of
the dramatist and the priest in the possibility of man's
triumphing over his environment. By Pelagianism I mean the
effort of man in the "secular city" to attain righteousness
through his own free will. By Manichaeanism I mean the
human effort to overcome the limitations of matter through
intellect. When I do use these terms, I use them positively
as manifestations of man's evolutionary growth and the convergence of intellectual, aesthetic, and spiritual powers.
When I use them, I use them in the same way Father Lynch
did, that is, rather loosely as convenient if extreme ways of
labeling certain human tendencies that are very much a part
of our climate of opinion. The alternative position of Christian acquiescence before the anomalies of the moral and
physical order seemingly recommended by Father Lynch could
with equal looseness be labeled as a kind of secular despair.

However, my task in this book is not to prove Father Lynch
guilty of an unforgivable sin or to present any of the figures
dealt with as champions of heresy. The voices are not those
of controversy but of convergence, a chorus of voices from
a variety of human endeavors whose messages, when drawn
together, give very palpable grounds for the hope that man
may reach, through improved technology and stimulated
imagination, new levels in his evolution. What Father Lynch
saw as the wrong-headed attempt to discover "new, extraordinary and incalculable energies in man," I accept as very
much a de facto tendency and the promise of human realization. In the words of Buckminster Fuller as he attempted
to envisage the next thirty-two years of our century: "We
are engulfed in an invisible tidal wave that, as it draws away,
will leave all humanity, if it survives, cast up upon the Island

of Success, uncomprehending of how it has all happened."[2]

Perhaps, in commenting on Father Lynch's views, it is unfair to quote from an article which he wrote fifteen years ago. Still the theological and philosophical battle with these heresies has raged — give or take a few centuries — for fifteen hundred years. It would seem about time to admit that they are sometimes used to condemn splendid aspirations in man. In Protestantism, Harvey Cox's *The Secular City* manages to avoid using the pejorative labels while extolling the tendencies. For that matter, Father Lynch may have changed his mind long ago — his book, *Christ and Apollo*, would indicate as much — but the stand he took is one that has been and continues to be very much a part of conservative and traditional thinking in and out of the church. I have not set up a straw man for the quick "sniker-snak" of my liberal sword. One has only to read a copy of the new Catholic weekly, *Twin Circle*, which labels itself as "a positive antidote to modern secularism," to see how ready some still are in the church to label heretical anything they don't understand.

Though every one of the technological and/or imaginative "heretics" dealt with in the following chapters denies the tragic inevitability of failure in man's secular attempts to transcend the here and now, every one of them in discussing the failure of humanity echoes Fuller's "If it survives." They do not see the characteristics of man and nature as irreducible, but neither do they see them as leading to inevitable triumph. Much — perhaps everything — depends on man's vision of himself. The ultimate heresy would be to hold that man had no grounds on this earth for a vision of happiness.

---

[2] Buckminster Fuller, "Goddesses of the Twenty-First Century," *Saturday Review* (March 2, 1968), 46.

Contents

Acknowledgments   vii

Preface   ix

  I   The Heralds of Convergence: Teilhard and Shaw   1

 II   The Secular City: Fuller, Bazelon, and Cox   33

III   The Society of Immediate Communications:
      Marshall McLuhan   65

IV   Enlightenment: Watts, Brown, and the Hippies   92

 V   God Is Functioning: Buber, Bonhoeffer, and
      Dewart   133

VOICES OF CONVERGENCE

CHAPTER I

The Heralds of Convergence: Teilhard and Shaw

"A degree more of Contact with the Centre is more important than any progress in the knowledge of geology. In this restful environment I have the impression to expand internally and I become conscious of a kind of new light which has been burning in me. Never before perhaps did I perceive so clearly the possible meaning of the evolution of my internal life: the dark purple of universal matter first passing for me into the gold of spirit, then into the white incandescence of personality; then finally into the immaterial ardour of love. And never before did I realize in such a tangible way how much people around me are starving for the same light, which perhaps I can transmit to them."

Excerpt of letter of Pierre Teilhard de Chardin to Lucille Swan.*

BROADBENT: . . . What is heaven in your dreams?
KEEGAN: In my dreams it is a country where the State is the Church and the Church the people: three in one and one in three. It is a common wealth in which work is play and play is life: three in one and one in three. It is a common- which the priest is the worshipper and the worshipper the worshipped: three in one and one in three. It is a god-head in which all life is human and all humanity divine: three in one and one in three. It is, in short the dream of a madman.

George Bernard Shaw, John Bull's Other Island, Act IV.**

Pierre Teilhard de Chardin once wrote that "It is relatively easy to build up a theory of the world. But it is beyond the powers of an individual to provoke artificially the birth of a religion."[1] To which George Bernard Shaw might have re-

---

* From The Wind and The Rain, John Hollander, ed. (New York: Doubleday, 1966), p. 32.
** From The Complete Plays With Prefaces (New York: Dodd, Mead & Co., 1963), Vol. II, p. 611.
[1] Pierre Teilhard de Chardin, The Phenomenon of Man (New York: Harper & Row, 1959), p. 294.

1

sponded: "A religion is nothing but a common view of the nature of will, the purpose of life, the design of organism, and the intentions of evolution."[2] Both thinkers had a theory of the world and its development which was supported by a perennial religion that predates Christianity, that indeed has its roots in the archetypal imagination of the human race and that seems now to be forcefully pushing forward into the consciousness of modern man.

The two figures were almost diametrically opposed on the surface, and, as far as I know, they make no reference to each other's works. Teilhard was a quiet, retiring man, who worked as best he could within the restrictions imposed on him. He died in 1955 with all his theological writing still in manuscript under the ban of his Jesuit superiors. Their posthumous publication and translation, and their reception by scholars outside the Catholic Church, caused suspicion among influential Churchmen, and in 1962 the Holy See issued a warning to the faithful against "grave errors" in his philosophy and his theology. At first, his place in the Index seemed assured, but recently official Church opinion has begun to turn, as Father Teilhard's writings have become more and more influential among Catholics and non-Catholics alike. Finally, in July, 1965, the new General of the Jesuit order — a Spaniard at that — hailed Teilhard as "one of the great masters of contemporary thought."

Shaw, on the other hand, was a self-appointed gadfly who held that any truth maintained for more than a generation must be false. And long before Madison Avenue became identified with advertising stunts and public relations, Shaw had become his own Madison Avenue. Not only were his manuscripts published, his every word was promulgated by the popular press. Yet this man also died, in a sense, unread. At the close of his career, Shaw could write: "I have solved practically all the pressing questions of our time but . . . they keep on being propounded as insoluble just as if I had never

---

[2] Quoted by R. F. Rattray, *Bernard Shaw: A Chronicle* (London: The Leagrave Press, 1951), p. 177.

existed."[3] An exaggeration yes, but Shaw did write wittily about marriage, the family, education, science, capitalism, and religion. The wit was remembered but the message was lost in the medium. Shaw thought he was clever in sugar-coating his philosophic-religious pill, but the audience proved even cleverer, for they licked off the sugar and left the pill. I propose to offer you the pill, which may seem at times to have the properties of a lysergic sugar cube.

Both writers are certainly consciousness expanders, well ahead of their times. Shaw died in 1950, Teilhard in 1955, but the full impact of their thinking, the full range of their vision, is only now being given serious consideration. And it is a vision staggering in its range. The first and last plays of Shaw's "metabiological pentateuch," *Back to Methuselah*, which will be the principle Shavian work cited in this chapter, are entitled *In the Beginning* and *As Far As Thought Can Reach*. That range is equalled in Teilhard's *Phenomenon of Man*, which starts with the primordial vital drive in minerals and takes us to a heaven of total convergence.

For a number of reasons it is convenient to treat of these two men first in our efforts to listen to some contemporary voices of convergence. In all my fiction and drama courses, one of my major concerns as a teacher has been to make students aware that literature is pertinent to their time. My juxtaposing Teilhard and Shaw is an example of just such an effort. It is most revealing to discover such similarities in the thinking of an agnostic and a priest and to discover how vitally important that thinking is, whether you approach it from unorthodox or orthodox avenues. Shaw once said that he would give serious thought to the possibility of becoming a Roman Catholic, provided, of course, that they made him pope, but, like it or not, he is in the process of becoming a Christian theologian. It is Shaw's awareness of an outer blessedness working in matter and leading us to the inner "vortex of thought" which links his position to Teilhard's and links both their positions to such a modern theologian as Harvey

---

[3] George Bernard Shaw, *Where Stands Socialism Today?* (London, 1933).

Cox. Teilhard's vision may move toward the poetic and mystic as he writes of "the white incandescence of personality," and Shaw's toward practical reform as he has his defrocked priest, Peter Keegan, dream of "a temple in which the priest is the worshipper and the worshipper the worshipped." But to both creation belongs at the end of world history rather than at the beginning. In that sense they are both existentialists, racial rather than individual.

Their very dissimilarities of personality and approach underscore the universality of the vision they held in common. It is as though the truth was there if only we would open our eyes, and they opened our eyes for us. Others have come after them, but Teilhard's evolutionary projection is the most detailed and systematic; however, his is also a most difficult statement. I most certainly am not using Shaw's views as a pedagogical device to expound Teilhard's. Shaw provides interesting variations as well as parallels which give a fuller statement of the perennial philosophy. Still, by juxtaposing Teilhard's theory with Shaw's more easily understandable — but, I must insist, equally sincere — projection, I hope not only to confirm the relation between these two and the vital significance of their message, but to establish as well a relatively clear design for the following chapters in which figures are presented who are involved to a greater or lesser extent in only part of the vision.

What is the perennial philosophy that these two voices of convergence offer us? First Teilhard's version. I will present it in a succinct manner which can then be developed through extracts and examples after Shaw's version has been outlined. I hasten to add that nothing in this book will seem, on first reading, more difficult than the following passage. However, the entire chapter, for that matter, the entire book, is devoted to explaining the vision of convergence conveyed in this cryptic passage. So then, if I were to use Teilhard's own highly technical (and, on the surface, unintelligible) vocabulary the major ideas would go something like this: From the punctiform infolding of a hyperpsychized core capable of autoevolution, the thinking magma has become by anthropogenesis a noospherically concentrated ultra-cerebrated superbody with superorgans and supermembers which unless volatilized will superevolve in neo-time, by excentration and transhominization, initiated and sustained by radial energy, toward a single supracosmic, hypercomplex, hypercentrated, superpersonalized, uniconscious ultracenter or archmolecule, the ultimate convergence of Christogenesis and cosmogenesis, the Omega Point.

The vocabulary is idiosyncratic, but the difficulty is not one of willfulness or — as hostile critics have suggested — an attempt to obfuscate what is essentially puerile. Teilhard, as a respected paleontologist, found it necessary to invent a new terminology to describe the evolution he was becoming aware of, an evolution that escaped the narrow range and rigid terminology of his colleagues. It was an evolution that was leading to "the immaterial ardours of love" and as such it demanded the addition of a poetical, truly religious flexibility to scientific rigidity. To use Bergson's terms in *The Two Sources of Morality and Religion*, Teilhard's vocabulary is the result of a synthesis of fidelity and conformity, of evolving religion and precise science.   .

The message is profound and yet simple. I have friends who range from college freshmen to an eighty-three-year-old lady, all of whom have found *The Phenomenon of Man* difficult going but who realize nevertheless that they have been yearning for just such a light and that Teilhard could transmit it to them. It is a message as simple as the account of Teilhard one day coming upon a friend in a remote corner of the globe. Teilhard greeted him so warmly that the other expressed surprise. "Why am I so happy?" said Teilhard, "why, because the earth is round!" All is summed up in that all-embracive enthusiasm. Indeed this acknowledgment of the earth's curved and conserving surface is a refrain that runs through the thinking of most of the figures I will attempt to cover hereafter. For Teilhard, as for many of the others, the earth's circularity is a concrete representation of the double and interrelated concern that forms the basis of his thinking — communications and love. According to Teilhard — and I am now reducing to more pedestrian terminology the statement made above using Teilhard's vocabulary — the appearance of "homo sapiens" did not bring the evolutionary process to an end. Mankind, while ceasing to evolve anatomically, continues to evolve socially and culturally because the rapid development of communication media has facilitated an enriching, interpenetrating and overlapping exchange of knowledge. Just as molecules and cells combine in individual bodies, so individual human beings are now combining in social institutions. However, because of the limited area of our planet and the increase in its population, the human race cannot survive unless mankind unites in thought and love. Therefore, we may look forward to a day in which the human species will evolve into a single, new, conscious entity, one which will no longer be dependent upon a physical body. For Teilhard, the future direction of evolution will be to a point of convergence, the Omega Point, where men become truly one in God, united to each other in and through Him.

This joining, this converging at the point of an evolving cone of consciousness bound in the circle of earth, is Teilhard's central concept. It is an inspiring concept both to those beginning and those ending life's journey because it means that nothing of psychic energy will be lost. To me in the middle of my journey, it meant a startling confirmation of inchoate longings and speculations. I remember, as a high school student plagued with retreats and sexual guilt, pretending that Catholicism did not exist and that I had the opportunity of working out my own religion, like Shaw, I suppose, being my own pope. I would usually end up with an unwieldy amalgam of Omar Khayyam, Kahil Gibran and Shelley. But always there was the recurring tenet in my make-believe theology that sin and evil were but dross that had only to be skimmed from the growing structure of virtue. My faith was optimistic, for I was convinced that the Incarnation meant that matter was sacred in some way and that

God's love was seeking ways to draw good from evil, to raise man to Himself.

I suspect many others were members of my underground religion and that may in part account for the phenomenal interest in *The Phenomenon*. It develops and gives authority both scientific and religious to a truth that we all to some extent have known from the beginning. To agree with Teilhard is to agree that the real emphasis of Christianity should be on the effort, the thought, the virtue of the past and present which have a cumulative impact, or — since impact does not quite do justice to the concept — cumulative presence, which can only be seen as God realizing Himself in some way, realizing His love, in our efforts. To use Teilhard's own words in describing the Omega Point, the ultimate stage of the cumulative presence: "If it is to be capable of joining together in itself the prolonged fibre of the world, the apex of the cone within which we move can be conceived only as something that is ultra-conscious, ultra-personalized, ultra-present."[4]

It is not such a wild or incongruous pairing of opposites, as it might at first appear, to relate Teilhard's "incandescent light" with Shaw's "mad dream." Quite recently Warren Sylvester Smith in *Shaw on Religion* devoted his introduction to Shaw's anticipation of the religious views of Karl Barth, Paul Tillich, Rudolf Bultmann, Dietrich Bonhoeffer, and John Robinson to prove that Shaw as a religious thinker is far from dead. Smith prints Shaw's unpublished article "On Ritual, Religion and the Intolerableness of Tolerance" in which Shaw reflects his innately converging frame of reference by recognizing not only the need of ritual for some but also the truth that "he who calls his brother a fool for clinging to one of them is a fool himself." But he goes further when he seeks the dogma beneath the ritual and takes "mad" Peter Keegan's stand. Shaw anticipates Bishop Robinson's position when he approves Dean Inge's observation that "if ordination be refused to all candidates who do not believe

---

[4] Teilhard de Chardin, *op. cit.*, p. 241.

literally and unequivocally what they now have to profess to believe before they can be ordained, the ministry will presently consist exclusively of fools, bigots, and liars." Shaw's creative evolutionism as related to the secular world can be identified with the modern concept of Christian presence which seeks to humanize the world not by dominating or preaching, but by serving.

And there is also a deeply religious sensitivity in Shaw the person which is sometimes missed because of his public mask. One has only to recall his warm and thoughtful letters to Dame Laurentia McLachlan (*In a Great Tradition*, John Murray, 1956), to know that there was in him something of mystic longing. To those who point out that such letters reveal only an untypically sentimental Shaw cajoling a nun who saw *The Black Girl in Search of God* as blasphemy, I can only counter that there was in Shaw always a strong strain of the romantic, a strain which emphasized the value of the individual, provided that individual knew what he stood for. In "On Going to Church" Shaw gives a brief description of the secular city, a description which Teilhard, I think, would readily accept: "Any place where men dwell, village or city, is a reflection of the consciousness of every single man. In my city there is a market, a garden, a workshop, a lover's walk, above all, a cathedral . . . shewing me where, within the cathedral, I may find my way to the cathedral within me. At all events, the Godhead within me, certified by the tenth chapter of St. John, refuses to enter barren places."[5] Such a passage tells us of the centrifugal-centripetal movement of Shaw's psyche. His religious aspirations moved outward and dealt with the secular city — as do Harvey Cox's today — not as the source of evil but as the place where God is now making Himself known to man. But in man's attempt to overcome slums, malnutrition, poverty, disease and dirt, Shaw saw him also coming into an

---

[5] Shaw, "On Going to Church." Originally this appeared in the first issue of *The Savoy*, January, 1896, reprinted in *The Savoy Nineties Experiment* edited by Stanley Weintraub (University Press, Pa.: Pennsylvania State University Press, 1965), p. 3.

awareness of the God within him. And though Shaw might refer to that God as the Life-Force, Chesterton was right when he claimed that the only difference between Shaw's God and his was a hyphen.

In this chapter, however, I will limit myself largely to Shaw's self-styled "metabiological pentateuch," *Back to Methuselah*, which he considered to be his most important work, but which is surely his most unproduced and perhaps unread work. Shaw himself was aware that with its five plays running at least three evenings, it was not likely to be a box-office smash. When Barry Jackson requested permission to stage the series of plays, Shaw asked: "Is your family provided for?"

Briefly, in this series of dramas Shaw puts his theory of the Life-Force to the test. His seems to be a dualistic metaphysics in which Life and Matter are the two basic realities. The cosmic drama begins "In the Beginning," when Life, hitherto "a whirlpool in pure force," enters into Matter and assumes the familiar shapes of the vegetable, animal, and human world. The fall of Adam and Eve is seen as a "felix culpa," forcing man to work out his own salvation, forcing him to ask himself why he has immersed himself in matter and willed to die. In the second drama, which takes place in the 1920's, we find that man has exhausted the benefits of the "felix culpa." Consequently "The Gospel of the Brothers Barnabas" is a plea for converging scientific and religious insights to regain the original unity of the Life-Force, but on a higher level. "The Thing Happens" is Part III. The year is A.D. 2170 and man amidst his futuristic and vacuous comforts is dissatisfied enough, in two cases at least, to will to live for three hundred years, thus facing the consequences of his actions as an adult. This section is not quite so absurd as it at first may seem. I hope to point out how it may be read more sympathetically in conjunction with Teilhard's theory of the growing noosphere. In the fourth play, "The Tragedy of an Elderly Gentleman," we are projected to the year 3000. The Elderly Gentleman (Shaw?) is contrasted with the world of "Long-livers" who find it necessary to put him out of his

misery of pettiness and narrowness. Finally, in "As Far As
Thought Can Reach," we are presented with beings who free
themselves entirely of their need for bodies. Matter has been
enslaved by Life, and Death abolished. Immortality has been
achieved and Life is pure thought.

It sounds like science-fiction. It sounded even more
unlikely in 1921. Teilhard's theory of ultimate convergence
must also have seemed strange even to him, held a virtual
prisoner of war in China, while Fascism circled the globe with
iron and death rather than with communications and love.
But with the thought of both Shaw and Teilhard we are in
the presence of vast and daring works of extrapolation rather
than rigorous systems. Their thoughts seem more feasible in
the context of modern technology, modern communications
systems, and consequent upon these, the growing awareness
by individuals and by groups of the desirability, indeed the
need, for interrelations. But the extrapolation has its base in
the past.

Both Teilhard and Shaw were evolutionists; both had
tendencies to "pantheism," and in both we find *inclinations*
to a Manichaean view of matter and to a Pelagian or semi-
Pelagian view of man.

In using these terms I certainly do not want to have Teilhard reconsidered for inclusion in the Index (I would like
to stress that "pantheism," "Manichaeanism," and "Pelagianism" were *tendencies* in his thought). However, the parallels
to Shaw are there. Though Teilhard does not equate evil with
matter (Manichaeanism), he affirms that a separation of spirit
and matter ultimately must take place and that "salvation"
will be realized through the invention and will of man (here
we see a tendency toward Pelagianism). Probably Teilhard's
crucial reservation is in his understanding of what he refers
to as "an absolutely legitimate pantheism," i.e., a form of immanence in which we have not "God becoming all" but
"God all in everyone."

It is as though material creation were a glove and God's
hand was in that glove giving it shape and possible move-

ment. God exists outside the glove and is transcendent, but he also exists inside the glove and therefore is immanent. Man must learn that matter is only a glove concealing the reality of God's hand from him, but the only way he can do this is by moving the glove in actions he "knows" are good and thus permitting God to manifest Himself.

Such an analogy is a simplification, of course. For the time being it is enough to say that both men — whether orthodox or heterodox — were disturbed by the growing rift between science and religion, matter and spirit, and that each attempted to reconcile this dichotomy by projecting a vision that encompasses time and space from "in the beginning" to "as far as thought can reach." Teilhard's *The Phenomenon of Man* can be seen as a scientific-religious realization of "The Gospel of the Brothers Barnabas" in Shaw's *Back to Methuselah*.

The evolutionism tending toward pantheism I find in both men is the result of a dialectic struggle between spirit and matter, a dialectic struggle which has its conceptual roots in the theories of Hegel and Marx. This is not surprising with Shaw. In conversation and in writing, he invariably used a Socratic approach in an effort to arrive at truth through contraries, and logically enough, in his constant attempt to attain truth out of half-truth and differing opinions — that is to say, in evolving his philosophy — he naturally was attracted to the dialectic method of Hegel and Marx. According to Hegel, God is thought; and as thought, in Hegel's view, proceeds in the dialectic manner (from an incomplete position, through the manifestations of the contradiction contained in its partiality, to a more comprehensive position), the process is logical and temporal. Hegel's dominant thought was the advance of history, in which he saw the groping ascent of reality, seeking self-awareness through the human mind, and trying to attain to absolute knowledge. However, the theory of Hegel was actually a system of rationalizing, teleological metaphysics, where all things have immanent purposes and ends which serve as objective criteria of evolution, and thus all his explanation is justification, all his history is theodicy. Evil is interpreted as the necessary counterpoint in a metaphysical harmony.

For Marx the subject matter of philosophy is not "the whole universe indivisible" but specific problems of man, history and culture. An answer to these specific problems may be recognized as true insofar as it enables one to settle the concrete difficulties out of which those problems have arisen. In the Marxian dialectic, matter with its concomitant evils shared the ambivalent role that matter holds in Shaw's and Teilhard's theories of evolutionary emergence. According to Marxian views of progress the old form of the state is not destroyed, rather it is assimilated. Even the original material has its purpose. Human needs are the driving force behind action and behind the plausible reasons one advances to conquer them. "Need," says Sidney Hook, "gives man his problems and the strength to conquer them. Need — 'the practical expression of necessity' as Marx calls it — brings human beings into consciousness, to class consciousness, to revolution."[6]

With Shaw and Teilhard the emphasis is not placed on historical, but on biological evolution. This led them nevertheless into speculations whose fundamentals parallel both Hegelianism and Marxism. The dramatist and the priest saw the development of matter and spirit, body and soul, as an interlinked process progressing in psychological and cosmological time. For them self-awareness was the cardinal need of man and the struggle for mastery of matter is essential in attaining that self-awareness. The four divisions of Teilhard's *The Phenomenon of Man* are titled: "Before Life Came," "Life," "Thought," and "Survival." In Shavian terms these divisions — preserving the same order — would be: "Matter," "Life-Force," "Man," and "Superman." For both thinkers the Thesis (Life or Life-Force) is progressively liberated from the Antithesis (Matter) leading to the mediate synthesis (Man-Thought) and the ultimate synthesis (Superman-Sur-

---

[6] Sidney Hook, "Hegel and Marx," *Studies in the History of Ideas*, III (1942), 336.

vival). However, neither Shaw nor Teilhard recognize absolute dialectic progression, for they refuse to believe that it is merely the interplay of contradictions which causes the world to advance. Their deep-rooted voluntarism simply refused to accept any form of determinism, historical or otherwise. They both postulated theories which made provisions for dialectic converging. Teilhard assumed all energy in the world to be psychic and of two kinds: tangential and radial. Tangential energy links matter or events on the same level of development. Radial energy operates at certain critical moments in the evolutionary process and tends to draw the known elements forward into unpredictable structures of greater complexity. This concept of radial energy is tremendously important in understanding Teilhard's thinking. Rooted in his belief in attraction rather than coercion, in fidelity rather than conformity, it eliminates the possibility of a senseless future in a closed circle of biological reduplication.

Shaw, too, held there was a law pulling life upward, an upward gravity going against the forces of entropy. He writes of this mysterious force: "I have called it the Life-Force and the Evolutionary Appetite. Bergson called it the *Elan Vital*, Kant the Categorical Imperative, Shakespeare the 'Divinity that shapes our ends, rough-hew them how we will.' They all come to the same thing: a mysterious drive toward greater power over our circumstances and deeper understanding of Nature." Again Shaw writes: "I, as a Creative Evolutionist, postulate Life-Force or Evolutionary Appetite seeking power over circumstances and mental development by the method of Trial and Error, making mistake after mistake, but still winning its finally irresistible way." The whole evolutionary view of both of them seems to be nicely summed up in Teilhard's statement that there is "an innate . . . preference on the part of the stuff of the universe for higher states of complexity and consciousness."

What of the "pantheistic" label that I have attached to the two men? With Shaw there is very little question. When asked "What is God; what is the Life-Force?" Shaw replied:

"When you are asked, 'Where is God? Who is God?' stand up and say, 'I am God, and here is God,' not as yet completed, but still advancing toward completion, just insomuch as I am working for the purpose of the universe, working for the good of society, and the whole world, instead of merely looking after my personal ends."[7] For Shaw the dream of heaven was of a "godhead in which all life is human and all humanity divine: three in one and one in three."

With Teilhard the question of pantheism is by no means as clear. He wanted to avoid the charge of immanentism but he also wanted to break from what he regarded as frigid, noncommunicative transcendentalism. He succeeded largely through the concept of radial energy or what can be referred to in this case as love, love moving through minerals, to plants, to animals, to men, to God its source. Teilhard uses the terms pan-Christism and Christian pantheism to express his view that the convergings of individual with individual and of godhead with creature were constant acts of love. Thus he thought that he clearly disavowed the pantheism of oriental religions which he felt did away with the tension of love by dissolving individual egos into a universal tapioca pudding. In his mysticism of love he "highlights the fact that union with God is obtained not by identification (God becoming all) but by the differentiating action of Christian love."[8] As Teilhard sees it "This is indeed a superior form of 'pantheism' without trace of the poison of intermixture or annihilation: the expectation of perfect unity within which each element will reach its own consummation at the same time as the universe."[9]

Actually the views of Shaw and Teilhard on this issue are not so very far apart. Shaw did not believe in the eventual annihilation of the ego either. In Back to Methuselah his ancients walk about presumably with cosmic thoughts on

[7] Shaw, cited by Archibald Henderson, George Bernard Shaw: His Life and Works (London: Boni and Liveright, 1918), pp. 477–478.

[8] Christopher Mooney, S.J., Teilhard de Chardin and the Mystery of Christ (New York: Harper & Row, 1966), pp. 179–180.

[9] Teilhard de Chardin, op. cit., p. 294.

their minds but freed from all savage instincts and, though united, obviously quite independent. But in neither case was this a concern about physical immortality for its own sake. It is interesting that Shaw, even in private letters, never mentioned dead friends or acquaintances unless their ideas and accomplishments were still a part of the contemporary scene. As with Teilhard, Shaw's concern was that man's accomplishments, his growing awareness, should be preserved. In this sense, avoiding the mystical, their "pantheism" can be seen as a commune in which, as Shaw wrote,

> the true joy in life [is] the being used for a purpose recognized by yourself as a mighty one . . . the being a force of Nature instead of a feverish selfish little clod of ailments and grievances complaining that the world will not devote itself to making you happy. And also the only real tragedy in life is the being used by personally-minded men for purposes which you recognize to be base.[10]

This passage finds echoes, I think, in Teilhard's sense of man's mission to realize the full powers of consciousness and ultimately to become incorporated in the Godhead. Teilhard writes that "the man with a sense of evolution grows immensely in stature. His life in a true sense ceases to belong to him alone. He comes forth, body and soul, from a vast creative labour in which from the beginning of time, the whole totality of things has been collaborating; if he shirks the task assigned to him, something of that effort will be lost for ever — lacking for all time to come." Teilhard obviously shares Shaw's dedication of the individual talent to the communal purpose. Moreover, he seems to be saying that this evolving collective superbeing can be hindered or blocked in his evolution by willful human beings who do not fulfill their duties. Of course when Teilhard finally discusses the end of evolution (the Omega Point) he sees it in the light of Pauline teachings which envisage the Church as a mystical body of Christ. But even here the wording suggests collaboration between God and man. In the Divine Milieu he

---

[10] Shaw, "Epistle Dedicatory," in Man and Superman, in Complete Plays With Prefaces, Vol. III, 510–511.

affirms that "all the good that I am able to do . . . is physically gathered up, by something of itself into the reality of
the consummated Christ." Moreover, Teilhard shares with
Shaw the sense that we must overcome our "feverish, selfish
little" egos before we can attain "the true joy in life": "A
tremendous spiritual power is slumbering in the depths of
our multitude, which will manifest itself only when we have
learnt to break down the barriers of our egoisms and, by a
fundamental recasting of our outlook, raise ourselves up to
the habitual and practical vision of universal realities."[11]

Both Shaw and Teilhard were very much aware of modern
man's disease or — using the word's etymology — dis-ease. Yet
they were both essentially optimistic in their views of evolution. That they could see clearly the evil around them and
yet postulate such theories gives added significance to their
message in our day. They both realized that without some
ultimate sense of purpose man psychologically finds himself
in a cul de sac of absurdity. In his famous Sorbonne lecture
in 1949 Teilhard insisted that what was needed was a "taste
for life" which had to be strengthened today in the depths
of the human soul, and that this meant fostering a sense of
some future issue through which our most precious achievements could escape forever the threat of total death. And if
challenged for absolute proof Teilhard was pragmatic enough
to say that "In the last analysis the best guarantee that a thing
should happen is that it appears to us as vitally necessary."[12]

That Teilhard could be so aware of our age of anxiety and
still be so affirmative is to me one of the most remarkable
aspects of his work. Based on dedication to a cumulative evolutionary purpose, his vision was always presented with enthusiasm well calculated to edify those of us who had perhaps
become willful and wavering particles of awareness:

> In us and around us, almost visible to the naked eye, a psycho-
> logical phenomenon of vast import is taking place, a phenomenon
> that came into existence barely a hundred years ago, and that

[11] Teilhard de Chardin, *The Divine Milieu* (New York: Harper & Row,
1960), pp. 127–128.
[12] Teilhard de Chardin, *The Phenomenon of Man*, p. 232.

may be called the awakening of the human sense. Men are beginning to feel that they are all without exception bound to an
immense task, the progress of which holds them under an almost
religious spell. To know more, to increase one's capacity: these
words, although to many they still have an utilitarian ring, are,
to most of us, haloed with a sacred significance. Men, today,
think nothing of giving their lives "for the advance of mankind."[13]

And with candor he presents his case for this evolutionary
optimism:

> If progress is a myth, that is to say, if faced by the work involved
> we can say: "What's the good of it all?" our efforts will flag.
> With that the whole of evolution will come to a halt — because
> we are evolution . . . We are confronted . . . with two directions
> and only two: one upwards and the other downwards, and there
> is no possibility of finding a halfway house. . . . Either nature
> is closed to our demands for futurity, in which case thought, the
> fruit of millions of years of effort, is stifled, still-born in a self-
> abortive universe. Or else an opening exists — that of a super-
> soul above our souls. . . . On neither side is there any tangible
> evidence to produce. Only, in support of hope, there are rational
> invitations to an act of faith.[14]

Shaw also saw the grim side of the present moment and its
ramifications in the future. His "The Tragedy of an Elderly
Gentleman" clearly indicates his distress at the inevitable
losses to be entailed in a long-lived utopia. And in every one
of the plays the collective progress of the species is delayed
by human willfulness. But Shaw saw himself as a teacher,
as a guru, who had a vital message to deliver. His tongue was
only partly in his cheek when he maintained that John Bun-
yan and he were superior to Shakespeare because that admittedly talented dramatist had indulged in the luxury of tragic
pessimism. At times Shaw's optimism narrowed down to
hope in the inexplicable appearance of the gifted individual,
the Superman. As with Teilhard he seemed to engage in a
Pascal-like gamble, to subscribe to an "as if" principle in his
theory of man's dedication. He wrote: "Creative Evolution
can replace us; but meanwhile we must work for our survival
and development as if we were Creation's last word. Defeat-

---

[13] Teilhard de Chardin, La Vision du Passé (Paris: Editions Seuil, 1957),
p. 241.
[14] Teilhard de Chardin, The Phenomenon of Man, pp. 231–232.

ism is the wretchedest of policies."[15] "As if," perhaps, but "as if" with hearty acceptance of the immediate fact of existence — and an existence that must not be wasted, that must be redeemed from insignificance. In this spirit Shaw unequivocally presented on his stage the individual as an expression of the Life-Force, created for the furtherance of a specific purpose. And that purpose — the criterion by which one judges the success of his life, is that by thought and effort, by contemplation and action, the individual seeks an ever higher degree of self-consciousness, an ever wider scope of vision, and, expressing life as life would wish to be expressed, seeks to raise the spirit to heights hitherto unattained. Philosophically, Shaw might say as did Samuel Butler, "I bet that my Redeemer liveth," but dramatically Shaw affirmed that there was a driving vital force behind everything, and in working for it, in forgetting one's self in a dedication to a greater cause, in the selfless acceptance of responsibility, man became more man, man became Superman.

Teilhard tells us we had better believe we are moving upward. Shaw tells us we must work for development. But what are we developing into, what are we moving upward toward? To talk about "goal" and "completion" in dealing with such theories is rather inexact. To say that this impelling and mysterious drive has a material purpose, has a conscious and preconceived design to work out, is, at best, a crude way of putting it; for to Shaw the whole process of life was an uncharted, creative and unending experiment in "becoming," and Teilhard's Omega Point, seen at least from a natural level, is not a final entity but a point of ideal merging of energy, and seen from an ultranatural level it is "an ecstasy transcending the dimensions and the framework of the visible universe."[16]

For neither is there really any definite end, any teleology. When dealing with final stages in their theories, it is best to use such terms as Teilhard's "genesis" or the more general term "emergence" rather than teleology. When the term

---

[15] Shaw, On the Rocks, in Complete Plays With Prefaces, Vol. V, 50 f.
[16] Teilhard de Chardin, The Phenomenon of Man, p. 289.

"genesis" is used by Teilhard in such self-coined words as "cosmogenesis" or "Christogenesis," it means any form of production involving successive stages oriented toward some goal. Here, of course, the goal would be in the one case the cosmos, in the other, Christ. But those goals are indefinable. All we can postulate about the cosmos is that there seems to be a pattern of growing complexity and consciousness directed toward the maturation of man. About Christ, Teilhard tells us that He is the Omega Point, the source of radial energy, of love, that attracts all things upward. The Parousia (or second coming of Christ in triumph) will take place at the critical point of human fulfillment, of human maturation. But the Parousia is dependent upon man attaining his maturation. "Christ needs to find a summit of the world for his consummation just as he needed to find a woman for his conception." Cosmogenesis and Christogenesis, creation and creator, converge. But Christ, of course, in His humanity and divinity is a mystery and what the critical point of man's maturation will be or how many millions of years from now it may take place is unknown. The convergence, therefore, is a matter of emergence, at least if one accepts A. O. Lovejoy's definition of emergence as "any augmentative or transmutative event, any process in which there appear effects that, in some one or more of several ways yet to be specified by science fail to conform to the maxim that 'there cannot be in the consequent anything more than, or different in nature from that which is in the antecedent.' "[17]

Note that in such a terminal convergence God must wait for man's "fiat" once again, that if matter is not removed it is at least glorified and transformed, and that man has in some sense merged with the godhead. We find the same variations in Shaw, too, when we attempt to establish his ultimate goal. In "In the Beginning" Shaw has his mother-nature figure, Lilith, invent matter which is but another manifestation of psychic energy (tangential energy?) so that spirit (radial

[17] Arthur Lovejoy, "The Meaning of 'Emergence' and Its Modes," *Journal of Philosophical Studies* II (1927), 170–171.

energy?) will have a force to compete against and thus realize
its possibilities. By the close of the play the evolutionary
struggle has resulted in the jettisoning of sex and time and
come to the critical point of discarding matter. They have
reached maturity. As one of the Ancients explains to the
younger Long-livers, man now lives enough to put away the
things of a child, and man's body is "the last doll to be dis-
carded." And finally in "As Far As Thought Can Reach"
Lilith, summing up the entire Shavian Pentateuch, can say:

> . . . after passing a million goals they press on to the goal of re-
> demption from the flesh, to the vortex freed from matter, to the
> whirlpool in pure intelligence that, when the world began, was
> a whirlpool in pure force. . . . I am Lilith: I . . . compelled my
> enemy. Matter, to obey a living soul. . . . Of life only is there
> no end; and though unbuilt, and though its vast domain is as
> yet unbearably desert, my seed shall one day fill it and master
> its matter to its uttermost confines.[18]

Shaw's He-Ancient probably goes beyond what Teilhard
would have tolerated when he proclaims: "I am the eternal
life, the perpetual resurrection." But Teilhard does echo
Shaw's Lilith when he writes that man "is nothing else than
evolution become conscious of itself. . . . Accordingly the
march of humanity . . . develops indubitably in the direction
of a conquest of matter put to the service of mind."[19] That
march, that process of evolution from pure force through
matter to intelligence is particularly meaningful when related
to the theories of Teilhard. In both cases God in a sense ful-
fills Himself in creating the world. He engages in a struggle
with Matter (the Many) in order to perfect Himself. This
ancient idea is found also in Boehme, Hegel, and Schelling.
Shaw's Lilith was in the beginning and is at the close. Teilhard's Omega has its Alpha. "Man only progresses by slowly
elaborating from age to age the essence and the totality of
a universe deposited within him." The pure force or energy
was in matter and was matter from the beginning but through
the years it became a "vortex of intelligence which grew

---

[18] Shaw, *Back to Methuselah*, in *Complete Plays With Preface*, Vol. II,
261.
[19] Teilhard de Chardin, *The Phenomenon of Man*, p. 220.

deeper as it sucked up the fluid at the heart of which it was born." For both men, then, evolution has been a process from a simpler form of energy, through the bonds of matter, to a more complex, yet unencumbered form of energy.

Shaw's Ancients constantly seek to concentrate their energies so that they may achieve their ambition that "the day might come when there will be no people, only thought." Teilhard, too, goes beyond the individual vortices of intelligence but he is much more explicit. Human history for him develops between two points of reflection, the one inferior and individual, the other superior and communal. At the close, with the Omega Point, the "individual" merges with the "community," though it still remains aware. Teilhard refers to this phenomenon as the mega-synthesis. Since this synthesis has a bearing on Shaw's ideas of ultimate convergence, I will quote a rather long passage from *The Phenomenon of Man*.

> Deeper than the common act in which it expresses itself, more important than the common power of action from which it emerges by a sort of self-birth, lies reality itself, constituted by the living reunion of reflective particles. And what does that amount to if not . . . that the stuff of the universe, by becoming thinking, has not yet completed its evolutionary cycle, and that we are therefore moving toward some new critical point that lies ahead. . . . We are faced with a harmonised collectivity of consciousness equivalent to a sort of superconsciousness. The idea is that of the earth not only becoming enclosed in a single thinking envelope so as to form, functionally, no more than a single vast grain of thought on the sidereal scale, the plurality of individual reflections grouping themselves together and reinforcing one another in the act of a single unanimous reflection.[20]

In writing of this "brain of brains" Teilhard says, "On this point I cannot, of course, force your agreement" but in a Shavian aside he adds that to accept this view "is eminently satisfying to the intelligence and strengthening to the will."

This thinking envelope, this noosphere, brings us back to the opening section of the chapter. Recall that I mentioned that all the implications of Teilhard's thinking could be drawn

20 *Ibid.*, p. 251.

from his enthusiasm about the earth being round. It is because of this circularity that tangential energy is able to produce "a harmonized collectivity of consciousness" or communication and that radial energy is able to lead to "the act of a single unanimous reflection of love."

The communication revolution excited Teilhard: "Thanks to the prodigious biological event represented by the discovery of electro-magnetic waves, each individual finds himself henceforth (actively and passively) simultaneously present, over land and sea, in every corner of the earth."

Shaw's group of plays has little to say about technological communication advances other than that fools are fools and with or without electronic devices they talk foolishly. But on the biological level he does seem to touch on Teilhard's theme in a rather amused science-fiction manner. In the last play in his Pentateuch we see children who have been in eggs for two years being antiseptically hatched at the age of seventeen. By the year 31,920 A.D. Shaw speculated in "As Far As Thought Can Reach" that the very atmosphere itself will be saturated with knowledge, permitting these young adults to learn in four years that they must go beyond science, art and sexual relations in search of the meaning of their own being. They influence one another in some extrasensory way so that the elders come when they are needed though they have not been summoned, and even the youngsters anticipate the moods and reactions of one another. Primarily, however, they seem to draw from a fund of information that represents some 60,000 years of man's evolution. After having been exposed to the communication waves of the elders for four years, the youngsters seem to complete that evolution themselves and are ready for what we can call in Teilhardian terms their "radial energy leap into the noosphere."

That leap takes us from communications to love, and again there are parallels to trace between the two thinkers. Teilhard's radial energy is love. Its source is Christ and its goal is the merging of individuals with Christ through their freely given love. Love, as Teilhard saw it, was the only emotion, the only force, in which we become more ourselves as we lose ourselves in others. Thus the ultimate convergence Teilhard saw was not a mindless mass but a vibrant interrelating of individuals. To attain this unity in the noosphere which is its destiny, mankind's power of loving must gradually develop until it is capable of embracing the whole of mankind and the whole of the earth.

However, "love is," as the song has it, "a many-splendored thing," and it cannot be separated from any other aspects of the convergence I have made reference to. Emergence, communications, synthesis, evolutionary theory and the origin of matter are all involved in this theory of inner development and outer converging. Thus, to plunge into this complexity immediately, the possibility of emergence seems inextricably linked with communications heightened by love. Bergson once wrote, in attempting to clarify emergence, that "There is no form yet, and life must create a form for itself, suited to the circumstances which are made for it. It will have to make the best of these circumstances, neutralize their inconveniences and utilize their advantages — in short, respond to outer actions by building up a machine which has no resemblance to them. Such adapting is not *repeating*, but *replying* — an entirely different thing."[21] Communication can be the simple transmitting of information which is repeating. But communication can also be dialogue or replying. Such replying demands being open to the source of your being and it requires the giving of yourself, which is in a minor way an act of love. This replying is the very action that mutually informs spirit and matter in the Shavian and Teilhardian syntheses mentioned earlier. The action is particularly clear in *Back to Methuselah*, in which Shaw adjusts the speed of his dramatic camera so that we can see thirty-thousand years go by in three evenings and sometimes in a few minutes see a person evolve from self-centered foolishness to universal loving wisdom. The dramatic camera is so adjusted that the

---

[21] Henri Bergson, *Creative Evolution* (New York: Henry Holt, 1911), p. 58.

results of the question and answer process can be seen exploding into fulfillment before our very eyes, like the trick photography that allows the viewer to see the full cycle of a flower's growth in a few minutes.

More particularly in *Back to Methuselah* the two human puppets, Ozymandias and Cleopatra, whose names suggest the futility of masculine power and feminine wiles, are portrayed as creatures who are incapable of love. They have no original impulses, are slaves of internal reflexes, are selfish, vain and totally lacking in self-control, dedication and a sense of responsibility. Being unable to contain effective amounts of Life-Force in their prefabricated bodies, they become "repeaters" rather than "repliers" in the vital dialogue and have to be destroyed. So also Teilhard refers to the "mass movements" of our times, "the Million in rank and file on the parade ground; the Million standardized in the factory" and sees it as the loveless "ant-hill of repetition rather than the dialogue of 'brotherhood.'" In spite of Fascism and Capitalism, Teilhard insists that "there can be no doubt of it: the great machine is designed to work and *must* work — by producing a super-abundance of mind."[22]

In such emergence, reality seems to be a gestation, a call, rather than a result that has already been achieved. With Teilhard as with Shaw the central preoccupation seems to be the effort to reconcile the directly opposite currents of entropy and life, and this is done by positing a dialogue between spirit and matter, between radial and tangential energy. That the results of this dialogue of love can be retained and become cumulative, from generation to generation, leads to one of the most controversial facets of Teilhard's and Shaw's thinking.

The views expressed above, flowing out of Bergsonian theories, are variations of the evolutionary theory of J. B. P. Lamarck which Shaw accepted totally and defended spiritedly and which Teilhard also found himself defending, albeit with reluctance and with careful qualifications. Shaw has explained how he adapted this theory for himself. He writes:

[22] Teilhard de Chardin, *The Phenomenon of Man*, p. 257.

Let us fix the Lamarckian process well in our minds. You are alive; and you want to be more alive. You want an extension of consciousness and of power. You want, consequently, additional organs, or additional uses of your existing organs: that is, additional habits. You get them because you want them badly enough to keep trying for them until they come. Nobody knows how: nobody knows why: all we know is that the thing actually takes place.[23]

To Shaw, to Teilhard, to Bergson, to Lamarck, it was always man who created the environment, never the reverse. This difference between design outside the organism and design within it is one amounting to a philosophic revolution. In contrast to the mechanists who would explain everything by material determination, Shaw and Teilhard are almost romantics in their vitalism. Teilhard seems to speak for both of them when, with the enthusiasm of a William Blake, he underscores the love convergence that takes place: "Object and subject marry and mutually transform each other in the act of knowledge; and from now on man willynilly finds his own image stamped on all he looks at."[24] The Lamarckian view enriched the human adventure and satisfied man's "rage for order" by positing a dynamic interplay between will (spirit) and matter which permitted matter to assume new shapes, which permitted spirit to develop new faculties. Immediately the center of vitality is shifted, the process becomes imbued with life and a kind of purpose which proceeds by infinitesimally small steps growing out of its immediate needs and desires. The process has no vision of remote consequences any more than the man who invented the kettle had a vision of the locomotive.

Of course, Teilhard's evolutionary views, as Bergson's, greatly modified the theory set forth by Lamarck. Father Mooney in his excellent study of Teilhard suggests that he was really converging Darwinism or the "without" of things or tangential energy and Lamarckism or the "within" of things or radial energy. "In evolution he saw not simply a scientific hypothesis, but an experimental affirmation of the coherence

[23] Shaw, Back to Methuselah, in op. cit., p. xiv.
[24] Teilhard de Chardin, The Phenomenon of Man, p. 32.

of being." Still in presenting his organic position so largely
based on the cumulative impact of knowledge and action,
Teilhard does seem to suggest strongly that acquired characteristics can be inherited and transmitted:

> The longer I pore over the problem the more firmly is it im-
> pressed upon me that in fact we are confronted with an effect
> not of external forces but of psychology. According to current
> thought, an animal develops its carnivorous instincts because
> its molars become cutting and its claws sharp. Should we not
> turn the proposition around? In other words if the tiger elon-
> gates its fangs and sharpens its claws is it not rather because,
> following its line of descent, it receives, develops, and hands
> on the "soul of a carnivore"?[25]

Such a view is totally accepted by Shaw. In "The Thing
Happens," the Archbishop and Mrs. Lutestring discover that
each has successfully willed himself into becoming a Long-
liver. And now well along into their third century, they decide to transmit their acquired characteristic. A typically
Shavian woman, Mrs. Lutestring is the instigator of consummation: "Have you time to come home with me and discuss
the matter?" Mrs. Lutestring inquires. "With pleasure," the
gallant Archbishop acquiesces. Teilhard is much more guarded
than Shaw and seems willing to substitute tradition for biological transmission:

> Under the free and ingenious effort of successive intelligences,
> something . . . irreversibly accumulates . . . and is transmitted
> collectively by means of education, down the course of ages.
> The point here is that this "something" . . . ends up always by
> translating itself into an augmentation of consciousness, and
> consciousness in its turn . . . is nothing less than the substance
> and heart of life in process of evolution.[26]

It is easy to see why in Shaw's view matter can readily be
altered by human will. For him matter was simply the invention of Life-Force and could be set aside when it had served
its purpose. Teilhard's view is much more qualified, yet
Shaw does seem to anticipate the scientist-priest's thinking.
Teilhard held that matter was energy (both radial and tan-

---

[25] *Ibid.*, p. 150.
[26] *Ibid.*, p. 178.

gential) and that in becoming increasingly aware of itself it was becoming transformed into spirit, into love. Teilhard certainly does not sound Manichaean when he expresses the force of love he feels: "Matter, you in whom I find both seduction and strength . . . you who can enrich and destroy, I surrender myself to your mighty layers," but he adds that he does this "with faith in the heavenly influences which have sweetened and purified your waters. The virtue of Christ has passed into you."[27] He can love matter because it is a means to fulfillment, but it is clear that if matter is worked on by spirit from the very beginning, if spirit becomes more and more freely disengaged, one conclusion follows, and that is that materialism for Teilhard, as for Shaw, is false. Probably Teilhard's views can be seen as orthodox on this issue, for they are a revival of the Aristotelian concept of matter defined as potential being. Still he could write: "I do not conceal from myself that this conception of a sort of positive nothingness, as the ground of creation, gives rise to serious objections. . . . It implies that the Creation was not absolutely gratuitous, but represents a motivated work of almost absolute self-interest. All this 'redolet Manichaeismum.' "[28]

"The motivated work" which is mentioned in this Manichaean perspective leads to the calculated and relentless optimism of Teilhard and Shaw which I initially found unnerving. My humanistic sensibility winced at what I considered to be the behavioral and scientific determinism evidenced in their willingness to tamper with genetics and to judge what was best for man. Both men seemed quite capable of resolving to decide "what medical and moral factors *must replace the crude forces of natural selection*," both seemed capable of leading us into a position which C. S. Lewis warned of in his *The Abolition of Man*. Teilhard has his human creatures seizing control of the direction of evolution, and Shaw has his "youngsters" fabricating human puppets and his "Ancients"

---

[27] Teilhard de Chardin, *The Divine Milieu*, p. 87.
[28] An unpublished paper of Teilhard, "L'union créatrice," written in 1917. Cited by Claude Tresmontant, *Pierre Teilhard de Chardin: His Thought* (Baltimore: Helicon, 1959), p. 92.

willing more body, less body, or no body as the impulse
moves them.

In the past few paragraphs, I have touched on the evolution
that takes place through the dialogue of love. The treatment
has been necessarily confusing, for that confusion is part of
the very dialogue: the lines of demarcation between subject
and object begin to melt and disappear the more intensely
we try to separate the polarities of the dialogue. This brings
me to the final, perhaps most difficult, certainly most per-
vasive consideration in this love-evolution.

To put it as simply as I can, in the convergence Teilhard
and Shaw envisage, the boundaries between self and nonself
break down. Recall the extract from Shaw's *John Bull's
Other Island* with which I introduced this chapter. Recall
Teilhard's insistence that in convergence "Object and subject
marry and mutually transform each other in the act of knowledge; and from now on man willynilly finds his own image
stamped on all he looks at." These passages are the very
heart of the matter, or perhaps I should say, of the matter-
spirit. They link to the ancient sages of East and West, and
I will have more to say about this in subsequent references
to Alan Watts, Aldous Huxley, Timothy Leary, Norman O.
Brown and the hippies, but they also link the philosophy to
the newest insights of philosophers such as Alfred North
Whitehead and technologists such as Buckminster Fuller.

Reality is a game of boundaries we play. We have willed
to perceive the world as a fragmented diversity, but unity
underlies all. For Shaw, Lilith or the Life-Force is at the
beginning and at the end of the dramatic game that goes on
for three evenings or sixty thousand years. For Teilhard,
Christ was in the beginning and He will have and will be the
last word. For both the true joy in life is getting outside the
game and seeing that you are part of a purpose that unites
you with all of creation.

Modern scientific thought emphasizes the physical interdependence of every element in the universe. Our two thinkers incorporate that knowledge, but go further. For Teilhard

clearly and for Shaw apparently, the energy that holds the elements together is love. It is knowledge of this force which is both the substance and the link of life that give purpose and meaning to life. At this point I am not talking about Shaw's 30,000 A.D. or Teilhard's millions of years into the future. Such knowledge of our immortality, in whatever manifestation it may take, frees us ultimately from absurdity and despair, but it also has immediate effects. Evolution must continue its gradual emergence, but the individual can have his moment of enlightenment at any time — a moment when he sees that we are all dependent upon one another, indeed interpenetrating one another.

Teilhard's passages on the physical attractions which become spiritual attractions are abundant and rhapsodic:

> Driven by the forces of love, the fragments of the world seek each other so that the world may come to being. . . . Love in all its subtleties is nothing more, and nothing less, than the more or less direct trace marked on the heart of the element by the psychical convergence of the universe upon itself. . . . Love alone is capable of uniting living beings in such a way as to complete and fulfill them, for it alone takes them and joins them by what is deepest in themselves.[29]

Shaw's expression of the theme of unifying love is, as might be expected, less lyrical, somewhat more specific and practical, but he does heartily affirm Christ as one who "advocates . . . the widening of the private family with its cramping ties into the great family of mankind under the fatherhood of God . . . and an organic conception of society in which you are not an independent individual but a member of society, your neighbor being another member, and each of you members one of another, as two fingers on a hand, the obvious conclusion being that unless you love your neighbor as yourself and he reciprocates you will both be the worse for it."[30]

The individual who does see through the multiple game to the loving unity beneath is released from the world of conformity and moves into an infinitely open world of freedom

---

[29] Teilhard de Chardin, The Phenomenon of Man, p. 246, 265.
[30] Shaw, "Preface" to Androcles and the Lion, in op. cit., Vol. V, 344.

and love, a world of fidelity. Abbé Louis Cognet can write disapprovingly of Teilhard that in his "thought the kingdom of darkness does not seem to have any genuine reality: the idea of man fallen and in bondage to the devil does not seem to be evident to him. In his system, evil is confused with the different natural inertias toward which man and the world lurch in their advance into the future."[31] This accusation reflects the sort of conformity, the compression of law rather than the expansion of love, that Teilhard fought against. Teilhard does not devote space to evil seen as the revolt of man against God under the impulse of Satan. Rather he sees evil as a disorder due to failure, to decomposition, to anxiety, or to the inevitable pains of growth. Evil is for him only a by-product of the essentially beneficial conflict between body and soul. The operation of "arrangement and centration . . . . . . can only be effected . . . objectively if it is rigorously paid for by suffering and failure, tears and blood . . . begotten by the noosphere on its way."[32]

Shaw seems equally disinterested in the concept of a God who keeps an accountant's tally of his creatures' peccadilloes. For Shaw, of course, poverty is "the greatest of our evils . . . the worst of our crimes . . . the vilest sin." He is not concerned with the individual's sin but with the social crime of "want" which inhibits human progress. Since the "sin" is social, Shaw refrains from presenting dramatic villains or presents them in a context of physical and economic necessity. Such sin is not forgiven through supernatural grace but overcome through the acceptance of human nature coupled with the attempt to perfect it by forcing the guilty to see the fact of their guilt in submitting to physical limitations. This "seeing" entails a profound sense of responsibility, an awareness that evolutionary progress depends upon each individual's effort to transcend himself.

The man who is able to see through the closed forms of appearance and morality to the essence of love beneath is for

[31] Louis Cognet, Le Père Teilhard de Chardin et la Penseé Contemporaine (Paris: Flamerion, 1955), p. 131.

[32] Teilhard de Chardin, The Phenomenon of Man, p. 311.

Shaw the Superman, for Teilhard the Seer. Teilhard can write:

> If to see more is really to become more, if deeper vision is really fuller being, then we should look closely at man in order to increase our capacity to live. . . . We have only to rid our vision of the threefold illusion of smallness, plurality and immobility, for man effortlessly to make the central position we prophesied — the momentary summit of an anthropogenesis which is itself the crown of a cosmogenesis.[33]

Such a "Seer" can anticipate the needs of evolution, can replace natural selection through "a nobly human form of eugenics. Evolution is in the hands of the creature evolving — or better, is in the brain." Through the conscious evolution of artifice, he can artificially perfect the thinking instrument itself. For example, he can develop computers which will not do his thinking for him, but from an almost universal pool of information will sort out and present the specific data he needs in making crucial decisions.

Shaw's Superman is also a "Seer" who has freed himself from the appearances of time and space, and has become evolution through anticipation, invention and decision-making. Shaw's Don Juan in Man and Superman refutes the Prince of Illusions by observing that life

> is evolving today a mind's eye that shall see, not the physical world, but the purpose of life, and thereby enable the individual to work for that purpose instead of thwarting and baffling it by setting up shortsighted personal aims as at present. . . . I sing not arms and the hero, but the philosophical man: he who seeks in contemplation to discover the inner will of the world, in invention to discover the means of fulfilling that will, and in action to do that will by the so-discovered means. . . . That is the working within me of Life's incessant aspiration to higher organization, wider, deeper, intenser self-consciousness, and clearer self-understanding.[34]

Such a vision motivates the whole of Back to Methuselah. Throughout the play, the dreamer, the inventor and the man of action are all able to escape the prison of matter to some

---

[33] Ibid., pp. 33–34.
[34] Shaw, Man and Superman, in op. cit., III, 627–628.

extent. And at the play's close the three aspects of the Superman merge in the Ancients.

The remainder of this book deals with what I consider to
be modern Supermen and Seers. Some are dreamers, some
inventors, some men of action or, equally difficult, men of
purposeful non-action. Most of them are controversial figures
as are, for that matter, Shaw and Teilhard. The seer usually
finds that the world is not ready for its saints, that law is
usually preferred to love. From the very nature of things, he
is always ahead of the evolutionary stage of his time and must
therefore violently and persistently challenge the accepted
categories of thought, canons of art, or rules of conduct current. Perhaps some of them will prove to be false prophets.
To read a man's motives is more difficult than to read his
texts. But all of them reflect in one or more ways the gospel
of convergence according to Shaw and Teilhard.

CHAPTER II

The Secular City:
Fuller, Bazelon, and Cox

The greatest poem ever known
Is one all poets have outgrown;
The poetry, innate, untold,
Of being only four years old.

Still young enough to be a part
Of Nature's great impulsive heart.
Born comrade of bird, beast and tree
And unselfconscious as the bee —

And yet with lovely reason skilled
Each day new paradise to build,
Elate explorer of each sense,
Without dismay, without pretense.

In your unstained, transparent eyes
There is no conscience, no surprise:
Life's queer conundrums you accept,
Your strange divinity still kept.

Being, that now absorbs you all
Harmonious, unit, integral,
Will shred into perplexing bits, —
Oh, contradiction of the wits

And Life, that sets all things in rhyme,
May make you poet, too, in time —
But there were days, O tender elf,
When you were poetry itself.
Christopher Morley*

The United States pavilion at Expo 67, the huge plastic dome structure, was a product of Buckminster Fuller's fertile brain. Aside from being the most imposing structure on the Montreal fairgrounds, it was integral, beautiful, practical, relatively economical and structurally sound. To that extent it was a concrete representation of Fuller's life-long philosophy both in technology and, by extension, in evolution. Fuller

* *Poems* (New York: Doubleday, 1925), pp. 203–204.

is the inventor of the geodesic dome which has been hailed as the greatest advance in building since the invention of the arch. He is also a philosopher whose mind bestrides the most colossal problems of life and living. The inventor and the philosopher converge, and in attempting to present this convergence I will use the adjectives I applied to the dome to describe the characteristic thought patterns of the man: integral, beautiful, practical, economical, and sound.

Richard Buckminster Fuller says of his technical accomplishments, "I did not set out to design a house that hung from a pole or to manufacture a new type of automobile, invent a new system of map projection, develop geodesic domes or Energetic Geometry. I started with the Universe — as an organization of regenerative principles frequently manifest as energy systems of which all our experiences, and possible experiences, are only local instances. I could have ended up with a pair of flying slippers."[1] In grasping at the universe, he managed to converge a great deal and in the process has ended up with something every bit as magical as flying slippers — the vision of a universal Utopia that is idealistic enough to appeal to poets and practical enough to win the qualified support of politicians.

Certainly enthusiasm for Fuller's ideas has been growing in recent years, particularly among the young. I suspect it is the "integral" quality of Fuller's thinking, together with his boundless, childlike enthusiasm, that intrigues them. Though he is seventy-two, he has accepted invitations to speak in almost every major university in the world, and wherever he goes students are his most fervent supporters. He offers them the hope of a new society built neither on the eighteenth- and nineteenth-century fallacy of reasonable perfectibilitarianism, nor the modern behavioral psychologists' plans for a mindless, instinct-conditioned society. Fuller sees rather "an entirely new philosophical era of man on earth." For the first time in history, he argues energetically, man has the

---

[1] Cited in Robert W. Marks, *The Dymaxion World of Buckminster Fuller* (New York: Reinhold Publishing Company, 1960), p. 7.

ability to play a conscious, active role in his own evolution, and therefore to make himself a complete success in his environment. Rather than the usual automated nightmare of hyperthyroid pseudoscientists, Fuller offers the poet's ideal presented in scientific language: "Progressive mastery by man of the physical coordinates of nature . . . may indeed be tending historically to permit the integral being of the child to remain unfractionated throughout the total life span."[2]

"Integral being of the child": I refer you to the Christopher Morley verses with which I prefaced this chapter. Fuller knows Morley well and he loves this poem. In its Wordsworth-like romanticism, it suggests a time when the child "came trailing clouds of glory," a time when the child was one with nature. For Fuller there is no greater gift than to preserve something of this sense of unity into adulthood, since it permits one to escape details and intuit overall laws. Fuller himself was fortunate. He reports that:

> I was born cross-eyed. Not until I was four years old was it discovered that this was caused by my being abnormally farsighted. My vision was thereafter corrected with lenses. Until four I could see only large patterns, houses, trees, outlines of people with blurred coloring. While I saw two dark areas on human faces, I did not see a human eye or a teardrop or a human hair until I was four. Despite my new ability to apprehend details, my childhood's spontaneous dependence only upon big pattern clues has persisted.[3]

Fuller maintains that neither he nor any other human, past or present, was or is a genius. Or he holds the alternate position that we all start out as geniuses but are "degeniused" by ignorant intimidation, lack of love, or unfavorable physical circumstances. Perhaps more than any other, the dream that motivates Fuller is the one of having mankind return to the garden of integrated senses and intellect. His technology and philosophy all point the way to that garden. When I saw his dome of Expo 67, it seemed to be a living unit. It provided natural light conditions, a controlled atmosphere in an area

---

[2] Buckminster Fuller, "Notes on the Future," *Saturday Review*, October 3, 1964.

[3] Fuller, "Man with a Chronofile," *Saturday Review*, April 1, 1967, p. 14.

of 6.7 million cubic feet, and in the breeze its nearly 2,000 variproportioned acrylic hexagons seemed to throb and breathe. Above all, the living integrity of this structure which Fuller calls a "geodesic skybreak bubble" is underscored by the dome's beauty.

Beauty for Fuller is an integral part of nature. He recalls that as a youngster in grammar school:

> I'd learned . . . that in order to make a sphere, which is what a bubble is, you employ pi, and I'd also learned that pi is an irrational number. To how many places, I wondered, did frustrated nature factor pi? And I reached the decision right at that moment that nature has a different system. . . . It struck me that nature's system must be a real beauty, because in chemistry we find that the associations are always in beautiful whole numbers — there are no fractions. . . . I thought, then the system will turn out to be a coordinate system and it will be very, very simple.[4]

Note that this sense of beauty flows out of a very practical, technical, mathematical concern. He is a friend of artists such as Alexander Calder and Isamu Naguchi, and he welcomes their enthusiasm for his work, but his concerns are not primarily aesthetic. Perhaps it would be better to say that the aesthetic and the practical aspects of his work converge to a degree never attained by the supposedly modern and functional Bauhaus-derived architecture of our day. In a conversation with Calvin Tomkins, Fuller remarked that "I never work with aesthetic considerations in mind. But I have a test: If something isn't beautiful when I get finished with it, it's no good."[5]

When Fuller attempts to explain his philosophy of technology and evolution it seems neither beautiful nor practical. It reminds one of Teilhard at his polysyllabic worst. The message of his lectures and his books often seems lost in the media, for Fullerese at its condensed, reverberating worst can sound like a physicist's version of *Finnegans Wake*. For example, he writes of the phenomenon of convergence — his

---

[4] Cited by Calvin Tomkins, "In the Outlaw Area," *The New Yorker*, January 8, 1966, p. 59.
[5] *Ibid.*, p. 85.

central concept — as "wave embodiments of cyclic experience which regenerate in the accreted morphology of nature's omnidirectional, convergent-divergent, synchronous-
dissynchronous, infinite plurality of pulsating controls of
interactive events in principle." This may at first sound like
nonsense, but such sentences should be read with as much
care as one reads a difficult poem. This figure, whom Frank
Lloyd Wright referred to as "a man with more absolute integrity than any other man I have known," uses language as
he uses material: he attempts to get maximum coverage from
a minimum of structure and matter. His sentences are canti-
levered by means of coiled tension rather than dead weight.
In the statement above, Fuller is telling us that nature is
made up entirely of energy, and that since the first law of
thermodynamics — the law of conservation of energy — at-
tests that energy can neither be created nor destroyed, it follows that the totality of energy is finite and constantly changing and overlapping.

Fuller's thinking is closely related to Teilhard's at this
point. Even as the Jesuit took delight in a circular world in
which energy kept overlapping and returning upon itself and
thus gradually becoming transformed through interaction,
so Fuller sees his "waves of cyclic experience" as "interactive
events." Teilhard does not use the word "event" in this sense,
but basically both the priest and the architect are in agreement with Alfred North Whitehead's use of the term,
"event," in his Science and the Modern World. Whitehead
holds that an event is a "prehensive unity," a monad which
when seen properly constitutes the ultimate value. For Teilhard, for Fuller, and for Whitehead everything is connected
to everything else in a great interlinked chain of being. Nothing is ever lost, neither energy nor matter, though matter, of
course, can be transformed into the other. These three thinkers perceived that wider pattern, as we, when a stone is
thrown into a small circular pond, perceive concentric circles
moving out in all directions and meeting the returning circles
bounced back from the shore. Our minds are able to grasp

patterns of energy — individual ripples — what we call individual things, what Fuller and Whitehead call "events," yet these apparently disparate things coexist collectively in a universe of cumulative and overlapping experience.

Though the sentence structures may be tortured and the vocabulary murky, Fuller's theoretical and global thinking is as well-rounded and structurally sound as the geodesic dome he invented. His genius may not have squared the circle, but through his efforts the structural soundness of the tetrahedron has been circulated. As Fuller sees it, the tetrahedron is one of the basic building blocks of nature's coordinated and beautiful system. His famous geodesic domes are essentially structures composed of tetrahedrons. A tetrahedron is nothing more than three triangles placed in such proximity that the base of the pyramid formed is itself a triangle; it is, then, a four-faced geometric figure, each one of the faces being a triangle. As a builder and as a philosopher, Fuller's rejection of the square in favor of triangulated forms is the central clue to both his practical and theoretical thinking. He delights in pointing out that for modern youth yesterday's "square-shooter" has become today's "square." This change in the climate of opinion, he insists with mock seriousness, is but another indication that the square is being displaced by the triangle as the basic form in architecture. The square as an architectural frame is wasteful and weak since it is composed of two dead-weight verticles holding up a dead-weight horizontal. But the triangle does not rely on weight or mass at all; it is, according to Fuller, a set of three energy events or vectors in such proximity that each stabilizes the opposite angle through tensile strain. When four triangles are put together even as a paper model tetrahedron, the structure proves to be amazingly strong, thus illustrating what Fuller refers to as "dymaxion structuring" — structuring that utilizes a minimum of compressive and wasteful mass while affording *maximum* and *dynamic* tensile strength. Such a structure can be nothing less than nature's basic building block.

As nature's building block, the tetrahedron turns up in a

number of diverse sciences. Where Einstein failed in his search for symmetry in a unified field theory, Fuller seems to have had at least qualified success in his hypothesis of the beautiful, integrated basic units of the universe. Molecular biologists, for example, have now established that his mathematical formula for the design of the geodesic dome applies perfectly to the structure of the protein shell that surrounds every known virus. Everything is connected to everything: the huge plastic dome structure shimmering in Montreal may be one aspect of an "event" whose feedback of insights could lead to a cure for cancer. Again, many nuclear physicists believe that Fuller's formula explains the fundamental structure of the atomic nucleus. Everything is connected to everything: since it shares the same structure, the living cell may very well have evolved out of the mineral, as Teilhard de Chardin had hypothesized. Thus we move from an architectural solution through potential solutions in physics and biology. But the convergence does not end there. Fuller's theories also provide evolutionary, theological, and political insights, that proceed directly out of applying the economic laws of nature to the human event.

"Economic" is the key word, not economy of money but of energy. In searching out nature's building blocks Fuller was attempting to find in science what could be used in technology for the benefit of man. He realized as early as 1927 that it is only through technology and fulfilled energy potential that we can disprove the Malthusian "law." According to the theories of the preacher, Thomas Malthus, life was an inherently pessimistic process of meaningless multiplication rather than of dynamic convergence. He held that the world's food supply grew arithmetically at best, while the human population grew geometrically. His view was seemingly confirmed by Darwin's theory of the survival of the fittest. Together, these theories provided a smug, religiously condoned justification for those who were "fittest" to regard the rest of the herd as necessarily expendable through starvation and war. It was God's plan. Fuller's life-long opposition to this closed, square, nonevolving view of man's future brings his thinking into the very practical area of politics, or better, into the more practical area of seeing through politics.

Fuller believes that our present-day machinery and processes of utilizing natural resources are "square." They are of such low-grade design that we are able to realize only four percent of the potential energy in a given task. The real hope for the future rests not in futile attempts to reform politicians, but in the increasing number of students who "are learning of the new and surprising alternative to politics — the technological do-more-with-less revolution." The seventy-two-year-old Fuller places his faith in young minds like his own, whose gaze may seem cross-eyed to the establishment but who are actually seeing integrated, long-range visions.

As Fuller puts it "Everything centers more and more on the young people, but they're up to it. World is going to work for world, that's all." He suggests "a world-around university students' elective research undertaking" to find ways of "upping the performance per pound of the world's metals and other resources." By increasing the overall efficiency of the world's mechanical devices from four percent to an overall efficiency of twelve percent, all mankind could enjoy the riches of our globe. Such developments as miniaturization of electronic equipment and a communication satellite weighing a tenth of a ton which outperforms seventy-five thousand tons of transatlantic cables indicate that the do-more-with-less revolution is accelerating.

In spite of the politician's firm commitment to starvation and war, man has continued to evolve. Indeed it has been because of war that the "haves," that the "fittest," found it to their benefit unknowingly to initiate the do-more-with-less revolution. Fuller points out in *The American Scholar* (Spring, 1966) that because of intense technological advance during World War I the percentage of "haves" rose by 1919 from less than one percent of humanity to six percent. "By the time of World War II, twenty percent of all humanity had become industrial 'haves' despite the fact that the population was ever increasing. At the present moment the proportion of 'haves' is at forty percent of humanity."[6]

If the human need to live well can replace the human desire to destroy, it is possible that one hundred percent of the ever-increasing population can become "haves." It is a matter of encouraging gifted youngsters to become "comprehensive design experts," that is to say inventors who will work out ways of replacing heavy, square designs with light, dymaxion ones. We are in a world in which eighty percent of all the metals ever mined are still being used. The metals are incorporated into structures and machines which, operating at full capacity, can take care of a little more than the forty percent "haves." Through inventions such as wireless, Telstar, the airplane, design experts have been able to make machines perform more services for more people while incorporating less metal. If humanity understood that the real world problem is not communism vs. capitalism but upping the performances per pound of the world's metals and other resources, we might be able to have a world of one hundred percent industrial "haves." It is not as wild a utopian dream as our "practical" Malthusian pessimists would have us believe. Again the important statistics: at present we utilize about four percent of the energy potential in our resources; all mankind could be "haves" if design experts could raise that to twelve percent.

In an article for the *Saturday Review* (April, 1, 1967), Fuller underscores the waste of the present political structure:

> Take away the energy distributing networks and the industrial machinery from America, Russia, and all the world's industrialized countries, and within six months more than two billion swiftly and painfully deteriorating people will starve to death. Take away all the world's politicians, all the ideologues and their professional protagonists from those same countries, and send them all off on a rocket trip around the sun and leave all the countries their present energy networks, industrial machinery, routine production and distribution personnel, and no more humans will starve nor be afflicted in health than at present.[7]

---

[6] Fuller, "Vision 65 Summary Lecture," *The American Scholar*, Spring, 1966, 217.

[7] "Man With a Chronofile," *op. cit.*, April 1, 1967, 17.

In place of the politicians' nineteenth-century laissez-faire policies, Fuller offers the dream of man transforming himself:

> There are many indications, however, that man is just about to begin to participate consciously and somewhat more knowingly and responsibly in his own evolutionary transformation. I include evolution of the environment as a major part of the evolution of humanity. In his unconscious participation in the past he has carelessly ruptured his earth, polluted his air and water, corrupted his children in order to sell any kind of toy guns, dope, smut and anything that would make money, and has made all money-making sacrosanct. But if we discover that man is necessary to the invention of the universe, we can understand somewhat better what he is inadvertently doing.[8]

I will have more to say about the practical, political implications of Fuller's thinking a bit later in this chapter, but the reference to the "invention of the universe" brings us to the "comprehensive designer's" universal vision which must be understood before its startling application to the secular world can be seen as logical and indeed almost inevitable. Man's intellect and the universe are the ultimate concern of Fuller. He sums up his philosophy of dymaxion intellect in a book which is significantly titled *No More Secondhand God.* I quote at length because the passage is of central importance in understanding Fuller's cosmic view.

> My continuing philosophy is predicated, first, on the assumption that in dynamical counterbalance of the expanding universe of entropically increasing random disorderliness there must be a universal pattern of omnicontracting, convergent, progressive orderliness and that man is that anti-entropic reordering function of universe and secondly, upon the assumption that man is born with an extraordinary inventory of faculties within an extraordinary inventory of universal phenomena. Most of the inventory is invisible, operating either infra or ultra to our sense apprehending. My philosophic working assumption goes on to assume that, despite the meager degree in which we consciously employ our capabilities in response to the meager degree in which we understand the universal phenomenon, we were given our faculties to permit and induce our progressively greater apprehension and comprehension of the universal phenomena. These assumptions are based upon what seems to me to be an overwhelming confrontation of our experience by a comprehensive intellect magnifi-

---

8 "Vision 65 Summary Lecture," *op. cit.,* p. 212.

cently greater than our own or the sum of all human intellects
which has everywhere and everywhen anticipatorily conceived
of the complex generalized, fundamental principles which all together interact as universe.[9]

Fuller makes no reference to Teilhard; indeed, his speculations in these philosophic, scientific, theological concerns seem
to have been formed at about the same time Teilhard was
projecting his own theories. Yet this passage from *No More
Secondhand God* has striking parallels to the priest-scientist's
The Phenomenon of Man. Fuller's counterbalance between nature's entropy and man's convergent, intellectual powers is,
preserving the same order, comparable to Teilhard's use of the
terms "tangential energy" and "radial energy." Whether it be
called "reordering function" or "radial energy," the phenomenon being described is the same: the human being grasping,
comprehending, digesting in himself the expanding universe at
least in a fragmented way, with always the possibility of
the individual gifted with integrated capacities of love and
imagination — the four-year-old, the genius, the saint, Shaw's
biological sport, the Superman — attaining a "progressively
greater apprehension and comprehension of the universal
phenomena."

The earth itself can be said to be anti-entropic since it
methodically converts star dust — cosmic rays and other radiation — into progressively more orderly organic chemical structures. But as with Teilhard, Fuller makes little speculation on
the stars and other planets. In fact Teilhard and Fuller, as
well as Marshall McLuhan, the communication theorist,
whose views I will grapple with in the next chapter, all
prefer to think of the earth in terms of a closed circle.
Teilhard refers to rocket travel only in passing; Fuller
has little to say about it as yet, other than to remind us
that we earthlings are on a rocket-like trip in our orbit
round the sun; and McLuhan is interested in space flights
presumably because they give man the necessary aesthetic
distancing to permit him to look back upon the earth

---

[9] Buckminster Fuller, *No More Secondhand God* (Carbondale, Illinois:
Southern Illinois University Press, 1963), p. v.

as a "pop art object." All of them rejoice that the earth is round and enveloped by its own atmosphere, for thus the energy supply is preserved. The energy may be preserved but it is not static. Fuller refers to energy "feed-back"; McLuhan uses the phrase, an "implosion of knowledge"; Teilhard writes of the "infolding of a hyperpsychised core." In each case they are describing a convergent energy which, permeated with experience, moves to another stage through man's circularly overlapping cerebration.

Fuller's "continuing philosophy" and Teilhard's perennial philosophy concede that the universe may be entropic, but the earth and man are the universe's necessary complement. None of the anti-entropic sorters on earth compare to brain-driven man who continually differentiates and sorts out his experiences in order to make generalizations and achieve more orderly and efficient patterns of action. Even as the physical portion of universe expands entropically, so the metaphysical contracts anti-entropically, and man's brain is that anti-entropic, reordering function of universe. Fuller sees the two laws, the two worlds — microcosm and macrocosm, man and the universe — merging. He defines the universe as the "aggregate of all consciously apprehended and communicated experiences of man." Man modifies the universe through his activities, but since man's awareness of his experience *is* the universe, man is modifying himself as well.

When Fuller writes of the "confrontation of our experience by a comprehensive intellect magnificently greater than our own," he is referring to what he described elsewhere as the "Universal, Intellectual Integrity . . . manifest to man by the integrated discoveries of experimental science [which] may be spoken of as God."[10] Teilhard's and Fuller's thinking can again be compared. Teilhard's noosphere, which is the product of the gradually integrating thoughts and actions of man, is finally realized in the Omega Point, in Christ Himself. Fuller, in turn, tells us that there is a cumulative field of knowledge which "discloses an *a priori*, anticipatory,

[10] "Man With a Chronofile," *op. cit.,* p. 18.

amorphous, and only intellectually conceivable, omni-integrity of universe."[11] Though this statement might seem to indicate otherwise, I don't think that Fuller holds that the final outcome of the universe is teleological. I believe that with Teilhard he envisages an emergent universe. There are building blocks, there are simple and beautiful laws which we can and must discover if we intend to continue our invention of the universe, but the outcome is unpredictable.

The slowly accumulating total world experience, the universe itself, is contained in the awareness of what Fuller refers to as the "continuous man" who represents "a world-around interlinked and continuously intercommunicating continuity of consciousness." Again Teilhard's noosphere comes to mind. Perhaps with its emphasis upon communication and technology, the concept of the continuous man should also be seen as another way of expressing McLuhan's global tribe of simultaneous sense perception. McLuhan goes back to the unfractionated tribal imagination for his metaphor; Teilhard goes back to Saint Paul's teachings about the body of Christ; Fuller uses the four-year-old mentality to convey his idea of the ideal man. However, all of them are projecting an essentially romantic concept. This continuous, global, noospheric man resembles William Blake's archetypal Albion who symbolized for that romantic poet man before the Fall and before the subsequent disintegration of his senses and faculties. The story being told by Blake as well as by the three modern thinkers is, in final analysis, the age-old tale of the "rite de passage." Once upon a time there was the original Garden of Paradise when the animal that was to become man was still in his preintellectual state of integration with his environment. He evolved a rational brain through feedback, implosion or the drive of radial energy and is now in the state of experience where he feels almost constantly a sense of frustration and alienation as he does battle with the "other": environment and minds not his own.

---

[11] Buckminster Fuller, *Ideas and Integrities* (Englewood Cliffs, New Jersey: Prentice-Hall, Inc., 1963), p. 230.

However, his salvation may be attained by incorporating this experience with the intuitions of the earlier innocence and through this marriage of heaven and hell, through this symphony of songs of innocence and experience, arrive at a state of global integration, and live happily ever after. Of course this Paradise Regained has its sexual implications, but that aspect will be dealt with in the chapter on Watts and the Hippies.

The attainment of the last stage depends upon man. This continuous figure is Fuller's personification of the unfragmented totality, the universal consciousness, collective memory and comprehensive experience which mankind must regain to attain Eden. Up to now the process of modification has been haphazard, but we must increasingly take responsibility for our image in the future. "The history of man," Fuller writes, "seems to demonstrate the emergence of his progressively conscious participation in heretofore spontaneous universal evolution."[12] Our advanced communication systems and industrialization, our mechanical extensions of man's powers, can now provide the capacity to remember and "teleologically realize" evolutionary pattern controlling.

Evolutionary design of man himself conjures up images of Huxley's *Brave New World* or that behavioral psychologist's nightmare, B. F. Skinner's *Walden II*. Teilhard and Fuller might recommend transformations in man's environment which would permit him greater liberty through freedom from poverty, fear, and sickness. Neither, however, would make the mistake of suggesting that technicians should play with man's chromosomes or di-oxyribonucleic acid. Teilhard was well aware that man owed his continuing evolution to flexibility, to adaptibility, and Fuller is in no danger of succumbing to the deluding charms of a prefabricated, preconditioned world in which man is treated as a thing manipulated by technicians and environment. He is aware that the process of modification must always remain to some extent unpredictable, since the characteristics of the end result of

---

[12] *No More Secondhand God*, p. vi.

combining diverse "events" are often different from and superior to the qualities of the initial elements. This variant factor he calls synergetic action, and, on the whole, he welcomes it as still another avenue of discovering ways to utilize nature's resources more effectively.

On one level synergetic action is a physical process. Thus the accidental alloy of chrome-nickel-steel produced a new molecular pattern with six times the tensile strength of iron and the capacity to withstand intense heat that would have quickly melted all three of its components separately. But synergetic action is also a mental process, a form of feedback. Thus for the past ten years the by-products of our efforts to do-more-with-less in weapons development have also had the unanticipated result of leading to inventions that have made living easier for many. There is an overlapping, a feedback of information from the various sciences and disciplines which almost inadvertently solve one another's problems. As computers — which after all are but technological extensions of man's brain-sorting powers — are fed the multitudinous information unearthed by man, we should expect ever-increasing problem-solving. Thus even an "anticipatory, comprehensive designer," as Fuller terms himself, would be absurdly presumptuous to assume he could extrapolate — let alone control — the future precisely.

Fuller's universal vision, in its emphasis upon energy potential rather than matter, in its efforts to do more with less, and in its fundamental position that intellect through utilized information will bring about the millenium, is essentially theological. Fuller uses the laws of physics to prove the superiority of metaphysics. Thus he can write of Einstein's famous formula:

> We are . . . confronted by a universe in which an intellect such as Einstein's could hypothetically take the measure of the physical energy universe, a measure which atomic fission later verified experimentally, thus demonstrating intellect's embracing and equating the integrated and differentiated energy of physical universe as $E=mc^2$. There has not been, however, either experimental evidence or intuitive suggestion of the reversibility of

those conditions and results whereby physical energy might take
the measure of intellect, equate and inscribe the integral and
differential equation of intellect and the metaphysical universe.[13]

As with Teilhard, the Manichaean and Pelagian tendencies
in Fuller result in a poetic and almost pantheistic perspective.
On this metaphysical level, Fuller is able to combine his
technical knowledge with a poetic extrapolation and postu-
lates an evolutionary step in which energy frees itself of
matter altogether and becomes a form of living thought not
unlike Teilhard's Omega Point or Shaw's ultimate phase of
man in *Back to Methuselah*. Fuller's position on his "continuous man" is more closely related to Teilhard's "noosphere"
than to McLuhan's global tribe, for he sees his composite
man as an "event" outside of time. McLuhan attempts to
grasp the changing electronic finite, while Fuller grapples
with eternity and the infinite. Fuller sees man, "superficially
challenged by the seeming discontinuity of death," surviving
through the communication of new insights to new life —
"the new life being spontaneously persistent, overlapping and
only modifyingly nurtured by the synchronous continuity of
old life." Fuller, in what he calls the "ventilated verse" of
his essay, "A Comprehensive Anticipatory Design Science,"
expresses his nonmaterial view:

Man is not a solid thing
nor is he the hundred or so pounds
of measurable energy, tied up in knots,
at any one moment.
Man is not the vegetables he eats,
nor the water he drinks,
nor the gases he breathes.
Man is pure abstract pattern integrity
made visible to other men
by man-tuneable frequency relays
of complexedly interlocking but
reciprocally accommodating patterns—
And man is the most complex of
individually differentiable
regenerative patternings
as a synergetic set of principles

[13] "Man With a Chronofile," *op. cit.*, p. 17.

> of periodic and accumulative behavior —
> as yet tuneably apprehended by man
> in all of his universe,
> with Universe taken to mean —
> the aggregate of all men's, all-history
> apprehended, and communicated experience.[14]

With Fuller's "mental mouthfuls and ventilated prose" we are on the furthest ramparts of his speculative thinking. However, it must not be thought that he is "forever blowing bubbles." The bubbles he blows are geodesic domes and practical modifications of man's environment. He proceeds from universal laws but applies them to particular problems. In conversation he observed that "In the universe, everything is always in motion, and everything is always moving in the direction of least resistance. That's basic. So I said, 'If that's the case, then it should be possible to modify the shapes of things so that they follow preferred directions of least resistance.' I made up my mind at this point that I would never try to reform man — that's much too difficult. What I would do was try to modify the environment in such a way as to get man moving in preferred directions."[15] At the present time, it is more than a "preferred direction." It is a necessary direction. Fuller holds that man is now clearly faced with a vital choice. "If he chooses chaos, he can go right on leaving fate to his political leaders. If, however, he chooses Utopia, he must get busy very fast . . . before an Oswald puts his finger on the trigger of the omni-inter-retaliatory atomic bombing systems."[16]

I mentioned earlier in this chapter that there were startlingly practical implications for the development of the new secular city if Fuller's theories about utilized energy potential are followed to their logical conclusions. They could lead to a moneyless utopia. I think we are on the verge of just such a breakthrough. Human nature may not be radically changing, but the rational invitations for evolutionary optimism

---

[14] *No More Secondhand God*, pp. 107–108.
[15] Cited by Calvin Tomkins, *art. cit.*, p. 64.
[16] "Vision 65 Summary Lecture," *op. cit.*, p. 218.

are ever more clear. Certainly President Johnson cannot be
considered an impractical dreamer nor the American Legion
a group of lyric poets, yet speaking before that organization
Mr. Johnson said:

> Unless we have the imagination to understand what is happening
> in the world, we may well find ourselves — together with our
> friends among the highly developed nations — facing a series
> of explosive crisis in which our military involvement is urgently
> at issue. . . . Only when we root out the very causes of war —
> the poverty of man's body, the privation of his spirit, the im-
> prisonment of his liberties — will there be a final surrender of
> violence itself.[17]

Of course this statement can be dismissed as a vivid bit of
rhetoric by a master politician, but the motivation for the
grand transformation proposed seems to be adequately selfish
and the means for that transformation are in our hands.

Fuller holds that:

> Comprehensive ephemeralization — i.e., the doing of ever more
> with less, per given resource units of pounds, time, and energy
> — has not as yet been formally isolated, recognized and discussed
> in print as such by any economists. However, as the years have
> gone by the combined effects of accelerating-acceleration and
> ephemeralization account primarily for the technical and econo-
> mic augmentations which are now overwhelming man — trying
> to make him a success in the universe despite his age-old-Malthus-
> supported conviction that humanity, regardless of its composite
> significance and fate, is, with but a few exceptions, destined to
> demonstrate personal economic failure, and premature death.
> Public policy the world around as yet assumes that Malthus was
> right — ergo, the vital necessity of Defense in view of the inex-
> orability of the next Great War.[18]

I agree with Fuller about the danger and the hope, but I
believe there is at least one economist who has been aware
of the "comprehensive ephemeralization" revolution taking
place. David Bazelon in his *Paper Economy* has furnished
us with a thoughtful appraisal of our money-myth society and
with a reminder that real wealth is found in human energy.

---

[17] *New York Times*, August 23, 1966, 1.
[18] "Man With a Chronofile," *op. cit.*, p. 16.

His theories of economy seem to me vitally related to Fuller's and warrant his being the second figure dealt with in this projection of "The Secular City."

Bazelon continues the intellectual revolution begun by J. K. Galbraith in *The Affluent Society* (1957). They both show that a potentially successful economic system, an object of almost unanimous veneration in the Eisenhower Fifties, had gone morally, aesthetically, and socially bankrupt. The system had become a conspiracy to sabotage the most productive apparatus ever created by man. Essentially they see that dismal and mean-spirited "science," classical economics, to be little more than a justification and preservation of the position of the "haves."

Bazelon goes further than Galbraith in making his points about what *ought* to be done. According to him the purpose of production in society may be either for the profit of the producer or the use of the consumer. In our society not only are the producers in selfish control, but the selfishness is compounded since capitalistic value or money (the paper in the paper economy) is only valuable when there is scarcity. The "haves" must never overproduce because they would thus surrender power to the government or to buyers. But we are now at a time when we could increase the 40 percent "haves" considerably. In fact, scarcity is no longer necessary in America. Thus we see that the pursuit of profit in the form of money leads to the deliberate creation of scarcity. In the light of such reasoning, it becomes obvious what we should do: production in society should be directed toward the needs of the consumer.

Of course the immediate reaction to such a theory is that dethroning industrial heads would undermine the capitalistic rights of the individual to possess material things. But in this "paper economy" what things do we own?

> To continue in our circumstances to speak of private property as meaningful and even fundamental, much less as the only basis of our liberties, is clearly an intellectual scandal. Most of us are

job-holders, paper-holders, and consumers — we control nothing
by property-ownership. And our present powerlessness is based
on and daily reinforced by the idea that we do.[19]

As individuals we produce less and possess less than we could
as a community. Bazelon, too, feels that a convergence of interests is necessary to adjust the disproportionate cut-throat,
competitiveness of capitalism. He is more severe in his
denunciation than Fuller. Fuller tells us that today 40 percent
of us are industrial haves, but Bazelon feels that 35 percent of
that 40 percent are the victims of short-term and short-sighted
planning which is for the sole benefit of the minority group.
He quotes W. H. Ferry of the Fund for the Republic, who
summarizes overall percentages this way: "As of mid-1959
. . . well over half the population owns 6 percent of the
wealth of the United States. The richest 1.6 percent own
nearly one-third of the country's material assets."[20] One recalls
how on October 25, 1929, President Herbert Hoover stated:
"The fundamental business of the country — that is, the production and distribution of goods and services — is on a sound
and prosperous basis." Hoover was wrong only because the
business of the country is not production, distribution and
service; the business of the country is making paper money.
Bazelon believes that if we could only clear up the miscon-
ception in our minds about what businessmen are really doing, and how things really work, we could then govern ourselves rationally and create an economic paradise.

This view that capitalism, with its competitive waste and
misplaced sense of values, must be drastically modified is, of
course, shared by Fuller. He writes:

> We now know scientifically that for the first time in history there
> can be enough to support continually all of expanding humanity
> at previously undreamed of and ever advancing standards of liv-
> ing and intellectual satisfaction in effective participation in the
> evolutionary process. But we are frustrated from realizing sciences
> by our different political systems and laws, which have all been
> devised to protect the few.[21]

---

[19] David T. Bazelon, *The Paper Economy* (New York: Random House,
Inc., 1963), p. 67.   [20] *Ibid.*, p. 337.
[21] Fuller, "Vision 65 Summary Lecture," *op. cit.*, p. 216.

Fuller quotes approvingly a physicist of Chicago University, John R. Platt, who, surveying general world trends and basic data, said: "The world is now too dangerous for anything but Utopia."[22]

But can Utopia be attained? Bazelon sees it as a possibility and, having disposed of the myth of money, he approaches the solution in the same way as Fuller. Recall that Fuller felt the do-more-with-less revolution had ironically received its greatest impetus through the two World Wars. Bazelon sees the second World War and its aftermath as an economic revelation:

> We may say that war is the most important illegal institution in our society. . . . It is so essential that, not having a real war to fight, we have invented a make-believe one so that we do not have to attempt the impossible and forego the benefit of it. Why? Because war is artificial demand, within the terms of the Paper Economy, and the only such that does not raise any political issues. The essential aspect of this artificial demand is that the *product* does nobody any good — only the *process* is beneficial: *war, and only war, solves the problem of inventory.* In the past, it was expected that resources devoted to war would be recouped by plunder in the event of victory. . . . Modern war is no such rational thing. The goods are given away. Payment for them would ruin the recipient: *vide,* German reparations after World War I. Further, one of the substantial but less noticed advantages of war is the opportunity after "victory" to give away more goods in order to rehabilitate the customer.[23]

As Bazelon sees it the immense production achieved during the second World War, both in armaments and civilian consumer goods, constituted an irrefutable demonstration that the industrial system could, indeed, produce total abundance. The United States, during those five years, produced 45 percent of the armaments used by the belligerents; this material was delivered to Europe and Asia, dumped on them — with no paper value compensation, and the result was a thorough modernization and expansion of the industrial plant. Moreover, production of consumer goods increased during each year of the War.

---

[22] *Ibid.,* p. 218.
[23] Bazelon, *op. cit.,* pp. 378–379.

If we can hold on to the truth that the process is beneficial and is value and combine it with the truth that the useful product is beneficial and is value, then Utopia is on its way. This brings us once again to Fuller's belief that real wealth is found in utilized energy potential:

> I'd realized that real wealth is energy, not gold, and that it is therefore without practical limit. Einstein and Max Planck demonstrated . . . that energy could neither be created nor lost and that it left one system only to join another. . . . And this meant that wealth was not only without practical limit but indestructible. Man's intellect, his ability to tap the cosmic resources of energy and make them work for him, had really caused wealth to be regenerative, self-augmenting. The main thing, then, was to use this great energy wealth to help man instead of to kill him.[24]

Here the universal vision and the practical application, the philosopher and the technician, converge. Since energy can be neither created nor destroyed, Fuller's primary wealth constituent is nondepletable. The other constituent, experience and/or knowledge, cannot create energy but it can concentrate it into new and unexpected uses. Fuller never tires of reminding us that the fruits of this real wealth can produce not only worldwide abundance but — in a sort of Sorcerer's Apprentice action of automation — reproduce the wealth itself by doing more with less.

Automation is of vital importance to both writers. This mechanical duplication combined with design innovations should fulfill the needs of all, no matter how the population figures soar. Bazelon delights in the dilemmas of industrial managers who wish to modernize their plants but who know that the increased efficiency resulting from further automation could destroy their paper profits. Bazelon's vision is limited to the here and now but I think he would agree with Fuller that a day may come — and soon — when wherever on this communications-interlinked earth a genius devises a way to increase our mechanical efficiency, a computer can be programed to duplicate the solution for the bene-

---

[24] Cited by Calvin Tomkins, art. cit., p. 76.

fit of anyone else at any other place having suitable equipment. Or the program for producing some desired physical item on a numerically controlled machine tool could be made to activate such machines at as many remote locations as desired.

This technology, this automation, is after all just brains. As Bazelon puts it: "We have reached a point in history where the noodle has finally come into its own. It now counts for more than force — indeed, effective force is now entirely dependent upon it. But it is not one man's brain. Veblen defined it this way: 'It is a joint stock of technical knowledge and workman-like habits, without the use of which the existing material wealth of civilized nations would not be wealth.' "[25] Automation, then, is a community effort; it is the institutionalized consciousness of the observable and experienced world. Both Fuller and Bazelon are in agreement that value is human energy, particularly intellectual energy, and that it functions with the greatest results when the society is a convergent one, one that works together rather than competes for larger shares of no value.

I suppose that it would be mere word juggling to attempt to fit Bazelon rigidly into my two-perennial-heresies theory. I have used his *Paper Economy* as a daringly conceived, neatly articulated statement that can be seen as a logical conclusion drawn from the speculations and innovations of Fuller. Neither thinker, as far as I know, has referred to the other in print. This, if anything, underscores the convergence taking place. Bazelon's theories about economics would seem to derive from the same climate of opinion, the same insights that motivate Fuller. Bazelon knows that modern man has it in his power to realize an earthly paradise through his own efforts, but that it is necessary for him to disburden himself of the dead weight of tradition. The economist does not seem to have the philosophic bent that leads Fuller to a nonmaterial, metaphysical plane, but there is constant reference to the converging community in his writings which

25 Bazelon, op. cit., p. 371.

places much emphasis upon that intangible factor, the spirit
of society.

When Bazelon cries out for an end to the wasteful, cut-
throat competition that characterizes our present fear and
greed-driven society, he echoes Fuller, Teilhard, Shaw and
the Hippies:

> For several hundred years now we have been experimenting with
> the first really big nonreligious society in the history of the human
> race. The results have been phenomenal for creative adjustment
> to objective experience. But spotty elsewhere: our souls are nearly
> dead. This untutored existentialism cannot go on much longer
> without leading to even more profound convulsions than we have
> already experienced. We are going to have to become more useful
> to each other as human beings: we may manage without God,
> but not much longer without each other. Without a sense of com-
> munity, society is absurd and detestable — and all members of it
> will detest it, somewhere in themselves, even if they do not kill
> because of it. Without community, we will have increasingly
> convulsive returns to de-civilized animalism.[26]

Bazelon ends his book on this note. He does not attempt to
suggest how that society would work.

However, in this cry for a religion based on a sense of community, Bazelon is also echoing — or more accurately, antici-
pating — the persuasive argument for a secular religion made
by Harvey Cox in his *The Secular City* (1965). Actually Cox
is not telling us how the secular society *would* work; he is
telling us how it *is* working and how, by accepting it more
fully, we can make it work effectively. He accepts the technological revolution reported by Fuller and he is in sympathy
with the needs for improvement outlined by Bazelon. As a
theologian, however, his own contribution to the converging
scene is on a different level — or levels. The converging of
theology and secularity, of Christ and the world, is his primary concern. As Cox observes, "Without a continual conversation with the real world theology itself . . . suffers. It
becomes effete, trivial and precious. Thus *The Secular City*
was written in an attempt to get theologians to open their
eyes to the secular world and to get those who inhabit this

26 *Ibid.*, p. 418.

secular world to understand it and themselves in a his-torical-theological perspective."[27]

Harvey Cox is in the tradition of Dietrich Bonhoeffer. Like Bonhoeffer he believes that we live in a "post-Christian" world and that the most crucial challenge to the Christian today is to make his faith relevant to the real world. He be-lieves that we Christians cannot simply affirm the reality of a transcendental God the Father; simply to affirm this is to evade our social responsibilities. For Cox it is God the Son who is specially pertinent to our time; the God who became flesh and blood and lived with us is the God who has relevance in our technopolis.

"Responsibility" seems to me the important word here. In the early years of the century, Shaw wrote that we must not accept the myth of vicarious atonement, that we are respon-sible for our sins and that only positive actions can balance or overcome the effects of them. To that extent Cox — as Shaw — is in the tradition of Nietzsche and Marx, for he holds that it is man who must become sovereign, man as a "free, creative, self-activity" (Marx) organizing and using power to subdue and express his freedom. Out of the struggle and discipline that this responsibility demands, the superman should emerge.

In a certain light his emphasis upon responsibility does not seem calculated to delight the average reader. Sociology and psychiatry, for example, are dedicated to shifting the blame for personal failure onto society. Yet such has been the en-thusiastic response to and continuing debate about Cox's *The Secular City* that the book must be meeting some deep need: the desire for a direct and cogent theology which is able to come to terms with the contemporary changes in society, science, technology. Bazelon's belief that the exis-tential *angst* must be replaced with a society in which the members accept responsibility for the needs of each other seems to be given voice in such a theology. The convergence

[27] Harvey Cox, "Afterword," *The Secular City Debate*, edited by Daniel Callahan (New York: The Macmillan Company, 1966), p. 180.

suggested has the sound of a noble adventure about it. As Bazelon puts it: "The sense of community is our expectation of the willingness of others. This is an act of faith at all times; and sometimes it rises beyond . . . to the proposition that all we modern existentialists have suspected and feared — that the alternative to religion is heroism."[28] I would submit at this point that Cox has caught our imagination by outlining a religion of heroism.

For Cox the Christian must stand free, without any traditional protection before God and before the world. He must be able to make decisions, take action, and assume responsibility for these actions. The modern man must be pragmatic and profane: "Life for him is a set of problems, not an unfathomable mystery. He brackets off the things that cannot be dealt with and deals with those that can. He wastes little time thinking about ultimate or religious questions."[29] Cox holds that we have moved from the ontological age to the functional age. The theologians must now deal with an ecumenical society rather than elusive universals. Cox's ultimate message would seem to be that enlightened politics should replace metaphysics as the context of human thought. As Fuller rejects the dead weight of the traditional architect's square, and Bazelon the restrictions of classical economics, so Cox would unencumber himself of an anachronistic past.

Frankly, such a rejection of metaphysical speculation disturbs me. In dumping God and the whole philosophic apparatus, I wonder if theologians of the "death-of-God" school (and Cox is loosely related to them) are not throwing out the baby with the bath water. My own reactions are closer to those of T. S. Eliot who wrote in 1932 that "The World is trying the experiment of attempting to form a civilized but non-Christian mentality. The experiment will fail; but we must be very patient in awaiting its collapse; meanwhile redeeming the time: so that the Faith may be preserved alive through the dark ages before us; to renew and rebuild civiliza-

---

[28] Bazelon, op. cit., p. 419.

[29] Harvey Cox, The Secular City (New York: The Macmillan Company, 1965), p. 63.

tion, and save the World from suicide."[30] No, I am not suddenly becoming reactionary in the midst of my converging liberalism. But Cox does take us relentlessly to the logical conclusions implied in the theories of Fuller and Bazelon. Cox is proposing that we accept the standards of a technological, nonreligious mentality and thus "renew and rebuild civilization" and in the process discover the essence of Christianity as well. Probably Cox is right in believing that religious language and religious thought in America at least are barren forms and that it is only by disposing of such language and thought the we can get to the religious spirit.

However, I will treat of the theological revolution as another manifestation of convergence in my final chapter. At present it is Cox's views on personal responsibility in a technological society that intrigue me. He begins his discussion with a quotation from David Bazelon: "The problem of the individual should not be confused with the problem of the corporate system, because we have already made our commitment to the latter." He shares Bazelon's uneasiness about the old guard administrator of the major corporations to whom "we delegate vast segments of our society's decision-making" only to have them "perpetrate the fib that we are still making these decisions ourselves, through consumption choices and shareholding."[31] Certainly heroes are necessary to combat this self-perpetuating, monolithic structure. It is not a question of replacing the huge organizations but of transforming them. Cox makes good sense when he looks hopefully toward "the rising new technologically educated class."

It is, of course, possible that this younger group will "sell out" or, gaining power, try to continue the old organizational ways. But the real danger is the male of 40 to 60, who has been brought up to be competitive and powerful, and who suddenly finds his power slipping away, because people don't really take orders anymore. He used to believe he knew more than the young; and he is coming to suspect that the young

[30] T. S. Eliot, "Thoughts After Lambeth," *Selected Essays: 1917–1932* (New York: Harcourt, Brace, 1932), p. 332.
[31] Bazelon, *op. cit.*, p. 174.

know more than he does and that many of them are not quite
as hung up on paper value as he would like. "The technologically educated class" of Bazelon is Fuller's new generation of "comprehensive designers" who would coordinate resources and technology on a world scale for the benefit of all
mankind. The conflict will be a violent one. Bazelon refers
to it as a "rather quiet and mostly polite revolt of the Intellectuals," but the Intellectuals should not be underesti-
mated. The old guard knows how to give orders and make
money; the technicians know how to make the machines run.
And it may be a losing battle for mankind. We have the
spectacle of our politicians leading us into ever increasing
armament buildups for our Defense Department, though
even they are probably capable of imagining what the results
will be.

Here is where the responsibility and the heroism come in.
I think that any number of the convergent signs I have been
pointing out indicate that we are on the verge of a truly
religious yet secular revolution. It is only a matter of people
having the courage to go ahead with it. We have already an
acceptance among the most dynamic and significant part of
the population on all levels that there must be a shift if we
are to survive at all. Now the catalysts are necessary. Change
has always been brought about by less than one percent of
the population. It is a psychological issue now, a question of
whether we have the courage to encourage others to fight the
old guard administrators and politicians, the courage to face
the technopolis of abundance ourselves. As Cox puts it:

> Man is summoned to be concerned, first of all, for his neighbor.
> In the age of organization he can only do this by getting into the
> fray, by losing a little skin from his own nose, perhaps even a
> spiritual value here and there, in the tough but epochal battle
> for the control of the organization. But as he does leap in, per-
> haps at the risk of his own life, he may discover that, even in
> the age of organization, precisely he who loses his life gains it.[32]

Perhaps the most challenging aspect of Cox's religion of
heroism is the call to play. The "job" is our security not

---
[32] Cox, The Secular City, p. 181.

only because it provides us with negotiable paper but because it affords us an excuse for living. It takes a brave man to be a playboy. Cox does devote the better part of a chapter on "Sex and Secularization" to *Playboy* magazine, only to castigate it for making a thing rather than a companion of woman. Yet later in a number of public interviews with Hugh Hefner, the magazine's editor, and in articles in *Playboy*, Cox seems to condone the magazine. I don't think Cox sold out. I think he may have lost a "spiritual value here and there," but he was really encouraging a necessary part of the secular revolution. As "a society living on the vanishing capital of a Puritan religious inheritance," we must train ourselves to be free, open, ready for all forms of experimentation in discovering who we are and what we want to do.

Secular man is challenged by the possibilities of leisure opened to him through *cybernation*. The word refers to the coupling of two previously discrete operations in our society: automation and computerization. Man has nothing to do in such an operation but program the task and service the machinery. I have already indicated in my discussion of Fuller the total abundance that could result from cybernation. It also means, however, that man need no longer work unless he wants to work, and, if this is so, the work becomes play. Cox holds that we are afraid to take the jump into the secular possibilities of cybernetics "because we have a semi-conscious religious commitment to work. Work is the religion of the posttribal man in the West. We are all addicted to the overpowering habits resulting from what Max Weber called the 'spirit of capitalism' and it is nearly impossible for us to shake it."[33]

Cybernation and its concomitant effect of moneylessness will release man from the obligation of doing other people's hack work, but there will still be in him the tendency to seek what Eric Fromm described as an "Escape from Freedom." Western man has to be re-educated, his childhood imprinting has to be changed. It may not be necessary for him to go on

[33] *Ibid.*, pp. 184–185.

an LSD trip, but he must learn to use his senses and his brain in a way he has never done before. This need, incidentally, is one reason I react negatively to Cox's antimetaphysical approach. Certainly the immediate practical revolution has to be accomplished, but we must also have a basis for existence after the cash-nexus has been removed. The alternative way of life is already being explored by the youngsters who have dropped out of society, by the artists who in our society are at best pariahs and at worst tolerated poets in residence, by the contemplatives of all types — including Teilhard, Fuller, and Cox himself. Such alternatives to our present way of life are play.

Cox's real contribution to the work-play discussion is his contention that "the most serious obstacle standing between the present definition of work and the one we need . . . is not political. It is religious." There has been a religious mystique built up around the interrelated notion of work-duty-money-salvation directly traceable to a misunderstanding of the biblical doctrine of vocation. In its worst manifestation it can become a national neurosis as described by Norman O. Brown in his *Life Against Death*. Cox draws together the need to abandon the old religious compulsion, the joy of the new freedom, and the responsibility of the individual engaged in his "play":

> As for how to use leisure, very little direct guidance is to be derived from the Bible since the possibility of full production with minimum expenditure of energy never occurred to the biblical writers. The Bible assumes that man will have to toil with the sweat of his brow, so long as he is man. But work and even sweat need not always stunt and deform man; they can also elevate. We must see past the historically determined form of a biblical image of work to its essential depth. For the Bible, man stands before his Creator and Sustainer as the one who is expected to exercise maturity and recountability in *all that he does*.[34]

As I have indicated, Cox quotes Bazelon's *Paper Economy*, but he does not state directly that we are headed toward a moneyless society. Instead he suggests that we should end

[34] *Ibid.*, pp. 189–190.

the present stalemate between production and distribution by bypassing the market and providing a basic income for everyone. "Then," continues Cox, "people who wanted to work at marketable jobs would do so and those whose interests and talents are not salable, such as poets and painters, would be able to live without prostituting their gifts. . . . No one would be compelled to do a job in order to share in the growing productivity of the economy."[35] Actually, I suspect that Cox is using the same stratagem suggested by Fuller who admitted that it was futile to try to change man's nature, but that you could so modify the environment that man would take the line of least resistance. The money economy is so deeply a part of Western thinking that to take it away abruptly would be comparable to taking away Linus' blanket. But if a community is created in which money is not very important, it may act as a transitional state. Again, I refer you to the hippie communities within which money is not necessary. Perhaps the question of whether or not the playboy of the future has play-money is not really of importance. Fuller, Bazelon, and Cox are interested in the full utilization of potential energy and this must be done through a community led by enlightened leaders who are dedicated to the fulfillment of the community rather than the needs of a few avaricious men.

In celebrating the secular community, Cox relies heavily not only on Bazelon but also on Robert Theobold, who in his book *Free Men and Free Markets* sings of the community where "we can now afford to say that if you want to cultivate your garden, if you want to improve the face of our cities, if you want to work with the culturally deprived, we will pay you to do this." I have no intention of exploring Theobold's views at this point. The triumvirate already represented provide quite enough material for one chapter, but I am intrigued that Cox should quote a social thinker whose metaphysical interests extend to Teilhard. In an interview appearing in the *East Village Other*, Theobold's impassioned cry

---
[35] *Ibid.*, p. 187.

for the noosphere underscores the fact that the thought lines of these advanced thinkers are converging, that the new community is ours if we will only subscribe to the "religion of heroism." In reply to questions about how to realize the new community, Theobold replied:

> I think we have to create Teilhard de Chardin's "Noosphere" in the immediate future. . . . I think that much of this exists already. Our great failure today is to recognize the reality that is here. The reason we can't see it is that we refuse to see it. . . . We refuse to call the noosphere into existence, because we refuse to create it through our own thinking. The old world of bureaucracies, the old world of institutions, the old world of order-giving is paper-thin. It exists because we pay tribute to it, because we believe it exists, because we accept that old world. The new world can be created because it's the good people in those institutions that matter today, and the power of those institutions, insofar as it still exists, can be mobilized by them. . . . I find that as one goes about trying to create this new world in which we become fully human, . . . one discovers it in all the most extraordinary places. But one has a leap of faith to make, a belief that it's there, and then it is there.[36]

[36] Walter Boward, "Interview with Robert Theobold," *East Village Other*, Vol. 2, No. 18 (August–September, 1967), p. 19.

CHAPTER III

The Society of
Immediate Communication:
Marshall McLuhan

Remember what applies to all my verse, that it is,
as living art should be, made for performance and
that its performance is not reading with the eye
but loud, leisurely, poetical (not rhetorical) recita-
tion, with long rests, long dwells on the rhyme and
other marked syllables, and so on. It should be sung:
it is most carefully timed in tempo rubato. . . .
Take breath and read it with the ears, as I always
wish to be read, and my verse comes all right.
           Gerard Manley Hopkins on his poem
           "Spelt from Sibyl's Leaves."*

Lead, kindly fowl! They always did: ask the ages.
What bird has done yesterday man may do next
year, be it moult, be it hatch, be it agreement in
the nest. For her socioscientific sense is sound as
a bell, sir, her volucrine automutativeness right on
normalcy: she knows, she just feels she was kind of
born to lay and love eggs (trust her to propagate
the species and hoosh her fluffballs safe through
din and danger!); lastly but mostly, in her genesic
field it is all game and no gammon, she is ladylike
in everything; before all this has time to end the
golden age must return with its vengeance. Man will
become dirigible, Ague will be rejuvenated, woman
with her ridiculous white burden will reach by one
step sublime incubation, the manewanting human
lioness with her dishorned discipular manram will
lie down together publicly flank upon fleece. No,
assuredly, they are not justified, those gloompourers
who grouse that letters have never been quite their
old selves again since that weird weekend in bleak
Janiveer (yet how palmy date in a waste's oasis!)

---

* Gerard Manley Hopkins, A Gerard Manley Hopkins Reader, edited by
John Pick (New York: Oxford University Press, 1953), p. xxii.

> when to the shock of both, Biddy Doran looked at
> literature.
>
> James Joyce, *Finnegans Wake***

I've heard Marshall McLuhan begin three of his talks with the joke about the mosquito in the nudist colony who said: "I don't know where to begin." Perhaps that is as good a place to begin this consideration of McLuhan as a "Voice of Convergence" as any. The world of humor, as a system of communications, is one that immensely interests him. He is delighted by the latest form of jokes concerning the "Poles" and gives as an example: "Alexander Graham Kowalski — the first 'telephone Pole.' " This kind of humor is like the type that the computer programers are reported to enjoy —"What is purple and hums?" Answer: "An electric grape." "And why does it hum?" "It doesn't know the words."

If you notice, the tendency in these kinds of jokes, or gags, is for the story line to be stripped off. They tend to be deprived of the old story line, and in its place you have a capsule, a compressed overlay, of stories. In fact, there are usually two stories simultaneously in these little jokes. The older-fashioned jokes had a straight, linear story line. The new stories tend to be much more compressed, circular in reasoning and simultaneously operating on multiple levels of meaning, like puns in *Finnegans Wake* such as: "though he might have been more humble, there's no police like Holmes." It is significant that in academic circles McLuhan is considered to be something of a Joyce scholar. Joyce's word play in *Finnegans Wake* and his use of double-plot in *Ulysses* anticipated much that McLuhan finds developing in our modern electric, computerized modes of communication.

But though McLuhan loves to pun, apparently enjoys the give-and-take of press conferences, and seems well adjusted to his busy public role — at least for a man who has spent

---

** James Joyce, *Finnegans Wake* (London: Faber and Faber, 1939), p. 112.

the greater part of his life in the "grooves" of academe — still his message is a serious one. His enthusiasm for the circular, overlapping joke simply reflects his enthusiasm for the circular, overlapping world, a world we miss in large part because we tend to translate the present immediately into the past, seeing all time always through a rear-view mirror. For McLuhan the unnoticed fact of our present is the electronic environment created by the new communications media. This new environment is not just a container for people; it is a process which shapes people.

In this chapter, as I attempt to clarify what McLuhan means by the new shaping environment, I hope it will become evident how wide-ranging is his vision. I see close affinities between it and that of another Voice of Convergence discussed earlier — Pierre Teilhard de Chardin. Teilhard was profoundly optimistic about the cumulative evolutionary purpose of the earth and saw it realized in part by the rapid advances in communications:

> Thanks to the prodigious biological event represented by the discovery of electro-magnetic waves each individual finds himself henceforth (actively and passively) simultaneously present, over land and sea, in every corner of the earth. . . . The idea is that of the earth . . . becoming enclosed in a single thinking envelope so as to form, functionally, no more than a single vast grain of thought on the sidereal scale.[1]

And Marshall McLuhan begins his *Understanding Media: The Extensions of Man* with these words: "After three thousand years of explorations by means of fragmentary and mechanical technologies, the Western world is imploding. During the mechanical ages we had extended our bodies into space. Today, after more than a century of electric technology, we have extended our central nervous system itself into a global embrace, abolishing space and time."[2] Whether they call it a "thinking envelope" or a "global embrace," both

---

[1] Pierre Teilhard de Chardin, *The Phenomenon of Man* (New York: Harper & Row, 1959), p. 251.

[2] Marshall McLuhan, *Understanding Media: The Extensions of Man* (New York: McGraw-Hill, 1964), p. 3.

thinkers are describing an intellectual process that goes beyond space and time. For Teilhard the thinking element is in the process of an evolutionary jump as extensions of its awareness, as its superorgans of communication, force knowledge which has been caught in the earth's curving surface to feed back upon itself. For McLuhan the emergence of electrically controlled communication media, the eyes and ears of the world, is now resulting in an implosion of knowledge. Knowledge and information envelop themselves multiple times, causing an experience of the information in depth. For McLuhan this is only the first stage of the electronic age. We are now moving into the computerized stage — the cybercultural era. Much as we have already extended our senses and nerves by various media, we will soon be extending the whole creative process of knowing through "the technological simulation of consciousness."

McLuhan has begun to pun on his famous dictum that "the medium is the message." We are now informed in the title of his more recent work that *The Medium is the Massage*. It is in the medium — punning is contagious — between the joke and the cosmic vision that we will find the full import of McLuhan's message. The medium area seems to be threefold: 1) history merging into anthropology; 2) an attitude toward education which underscores a new psychology of learning; and 3) a theory of sensory perception leading to a theory of art. Each is devoted to a different period of time: the past, present and future; thus, in view of the ambitious range of interests and time covered, one can see why his friend Robert Corrigan, Dean of the College of Dramatic Arts at New York University, refers to him as "the first heavy-duty philosopher of the mid-twentieth century, the legitimate article, a Descartes of the age of the computer." Though his range is great, the organization of material at times is almost hopeless. His medium seems to break down under the weight of the message and he becomes an elliptical Joycean joker or obscure Teilhardian visionary. He himself says, "I don't explain; I explore — to explain is to explain away." His favorite word seems to be "probe." There is little step-by-step reasoning in his writings; he communicates by multiple example. There is an all-at-onceness to his style; generally you grasp it all at once or not at all. He relies on metaphor, aphorism, wordplay to make his points, all time-honored devices for the instantaneous communication of complex ideas, and probably the only way what he has to say can be communicated. Language is his medium, and the way he uses it is a major part of his message.

McLuhan is slipshod in his composition. He dictates his thoughts as they come to him and seldom rewrites because, as he explains, "I tend to add, and the whole thing gets out of hand. Most clear writing is a sign that there is no exploration going on." Certainly McLuhan can't be accused of clear writing. Consider the following typical extract from his major communication statement thus far, *Understanding Media*.

> The movie, by sheer speeding up the mechanical, carried us from the world of sequence and connections into the world of creative configuration and structure. The message of the movie medium is that of transition from linear connections to configurations. It is the transition that produces the now quite correct observation: "If it works, it's obsolete." When electric speed further takes over from mechanical movie sequences, then the lines of force in structures and in media become loud and clear. We return to the inclusive form of the icon.[3]

But there is exploration going on in such an all-at-onceness passage, and it is an exploration that suggests the three converging avenues of past, present and future, of history, education and art. The significant phrases are "world of sequence," "The message of the . . . medium," "the inclusive form of the icon."

Historically and anthropologically McLuhan believes we began with a society of inclusive form, moved to a world of sequential form and are now returning to iconic totality, to a society of immediate and total communication. The first stage can be called the "oral-aural" or voice-and-ear stage, when all verbal transmission was simply oral. The second was

[3] *Ibid.*, p. 12.

the chirographic-typographic stage, which began roughly at the time of the creation of the alphabet and was consummated with the invention of the printing press. The third is the electronic stage of the present epoch. In his first book, *The Mechanical Bride* (1951), McLuhan anticipated much of his later thinking by exploring what similarities existed between mass culture and elite art, but it was in his second work, *The Gutenberg Galaxy* (1962), that he began to project his concept of man's environmental development. In this work he deals with the first two stages and in a romantic-pastoral mood dwells upon the loss man suffered through Gutenberg's invention.

In the original world of iconic inclusive form, prior to the invention of the phonetic alphabet, man existed within a tribal and oral pattern with its seamless web of kinship and interdependence. The chief medium for the exchange of information was speech, in effect a natural resource made equally available to all. No individual, therefore, knew appreciably more or less than the rest of the tribe. Hence there was no individualism and very little specialization. This earlier society may have been low in the amount of abstract information at its disposal, and therefore low in its ability to control its environment, but it had certain advantages over the post-Gutenberg period. It would not have been able to discuss alienation, deracination, nihilism or absurdity, but then it had no need for such terms since it was not experiencing such sensations. It probably had a sense of community we might envy and an inner life responsive to myth, to the iconic, to the unseen pattern of the natural world, quite a bit richer than our own.

It seems to me that McLuhan shares with the French anthropologist, Claude Lévi-Strauss, a desire to come in contact with and in a sense recapture the neolithic intelligence. There is a desire to converge with our past. In *The Savage Mind* (1966) Lévi-Strauss suggests that we have never lost the tribal mind, that it is immanent in us all. He writes that "if the [human] race has so far concentrated on one task, and

one alone — that of building a society in which Man can live
— then the sources of strength on which our remote ancestors
drew are present also in ourselves. . . . Human brotherhood
acquires a palpable significance when we find our image of it
confirmed in the poorest of tribes, and when that tribe offers
us an experience which, when joined with many hundreds of
others, has a lesson to teach us."[4] For both men, the best —
but in no sense perfect — time for man was the neolithic
(i.e., post-agricultural, pre-urban) age. For it was when this
mentality of totality flourished, when the images drawn from
myth, ritual, magic and tribal memory generally seemed to be
distributed in icons, in patterns, in symbolic structures capable of formulating and communicating objective analyses
of the social and physical world that those arts of civilization
were produced — agriculture, animal husbandry, pottery,
weaving, food conservation and preparation, etc. — arts which
still provide the foundation of our existence.

In discussing tribal effectiveness in our own day, McLuhan
mentions the Eskimos who have their own total way of per-
ceiving the world. "They have phenomenal memories. They
travel without visual bearings in their white-on-white world
and can sketch cartographically accurate maps of shifting
shorelines. They have forty or fifty words for what we call
'snow.' They live in a world without linearity, a world of
acoustic space."[5] Dipping into the past on a more sophisticated level, McLuhan refers to what happened in Greece in
"the tribal encyclopedia" period before Plato. The young
memorized the poets. The poets were operative purveyors of
practical wisdom and counsel. Homer, Hesiod and the rest
actually provided the young people with models of perception and models of behavior and strategies for overcoming all
sorts of difficulties and obstacles. The great Odysseus was
above all a Greek hero because of his resourcefulness — his
unfailing initiative and skill in every type of opaque and

---

[4] Claude Lévi-Strauss, *The Savage Mind* (Chicago: The University of
Chicago Press, 1966), p. 12.

[5] McLuhan, quoted by John M. Culkin, S.J., "A Schoolman's Guide to
Marshall McLuhan," *Saturday Review*, March 18, 1962, 53.

threatening situation. McLuhan describes this education
with poets as teachers, this tribal encyclopedia, and then
the advent of writing and the complete change that came
over education as a result. With the coming of writing,
education shifted from the memorizing of the tribal encyclopedia that made education a sort of "singing com-
mercial." With writing came the classification of knowledge, the ideas, the categories; and Plato's detestation of the
poets was mainly a rivalry with the old educational establishment, which had naturally failed to come to grips with the
new technology of the written word.

In the second stage, in the mechanical era, in "the world
of sequence," which stretches from the fifteenth to the early
twentieth century, we relied on the printed page. And as a
consequence, we started reasoning in a manner dictated by
the restrictions print imposes upon language. We started
classifying and categorizing information, thinking in a step-
by-step "linear" fashion. This kind of compartmentalization
(fragmentation is McLuhan's word) is reflected in our
political subdivisions, of nations and states, in manufacturing
processes — the assembly line — in our educational pattern
from the structure of the university to approved research
procedures. Moreover, now influenced by the alphabet, literate human culture became progressively more visual than
oral; it began to conceive of the universe and finally of the
human mind itself in terms of sight and of spatial diagrams.

In our culture, we are trained, generally during childhood,
to believe in the alphabet, a training which has disastrous
effects on the psyche. Massive repressions are set up, which
differentiate literate from illiterate man, detribalize him,
force him back upon himself, and encourage reflection,
analysis, and a large store of guilt feelings different from those
of illiterate man. Literate man often characteristically seeks
relief from his tensions in schizophrenic delusional systemati-
zation, setting up a self-consistent dreamworld into which
he can retire from anxiety. As McLuhan puts it, "When
literate and specialized people get into a state of stress, they

split themselves up into little bits and go to a psychiatrist, hoping to be reassembled. Primitive or integral people, on the other hand, don't split under stress, they go berserk. They react as a totality, like a charging rhino."[6]

The emergence of alphabetic typography is associated with the great intensification of spatial awareness in the European culture where alphabetic typography developed. The fifteenth and subsequent centuries mark the age of full linear perspective in painting, of maps and the concomitant sense of the earth's surface as a spatial expanse to be covered by exploration, of Copernican cosmology and Newtonian physics, which plotted the universe with charts more than ever before and reduced the old nature philosophy in the physical sciences to ineffectiveness.

The heightening of the importance of vision which accompanied typography changed man's sense of the universe about him. Vision depersonalizes. This truth can be grasped immediately if we reflect that to stare at another person, to treat him merely as an object of vision, is intolerable, for it reduces the other to a mere thing. One can, on the other hand, look at an individual as long as one wishes provided one talks to him at the same time. Speech personalizes. The movement from the old oral-aural world to the new visual world of alphabetic writing and typography can be understood largely in terms of this polarity between speech and vision. The old oral-aural culture was highly personal, nonanalytic, dramatic, oratorical, full of hostilities, some natural and some cultivated — cultivated, for example, in the practice of dialectic and rhetoric, to which the academic system clung for almost all its teaching, despite writing and print, until the advent of the romantic age. The newer chirographic culture, matured by typography, and at long last relatively victorious, depersonalized the world.

In *Understanding Media* (1964), McLuhan focuses on the third phase of man's environmental evolution, the electronic-

---

[6] McLuhan, quoted by Robert Corrigan, "The Brave New World of Marshall McLuhan," *Glamour*, July, 1966, 135.

computer age. With the electric circuit, everything changed.
New means of communication, new media, have taken over
from type. Print is still with us, but we have television, radio,
movies, as well, and they have changed the shape of things.
The new media feed information to electric age man through
all his senses, too swiftly and in too great complexity for
simple classification of ideas. The electric age is, as well, the
age of the computer, and to function within it, man must become a kind of computer himself. To describe his thought
processes, McLuhan uses the computer-metaphor "pattern
recognition" which is but a manifestation of a return to the
inclusive form of the icon. Electric-age man is no longer
fragmented. He responds totally to his total environment,
much as did primitive, oral man, many of whose attributes
he is taking on. Thus we are now involved in a new and at
the same time ancient convergence.

The introduction of electronic communication has re-
aligned worlds of sound and sight, so reactivating the world
of voice that contemporary technological culture paradoxically
resembles to a significant though qualitatively different degree
the old oral tribal culture of all mankind. We now experience
simultaneity in space and time. Events in Vietnam and
Washington occur to us through radio, telephone and television collectively and concurrently almost at the moment
of their happening. But of course the "global village" that
results from this oral collectivity is vastly different from the
village of tribal antiquity by the very fact of its being global.
Our present oral culture must sustain diversities and strains
on the psyche which earlier tribal cultures did not know and
could not have tolerated. But McLuhan does not consider
modern technology as an uncontrollable and inhuman mon-
ster threatening to consume man. Technology is but another
very human artifact that presents exciting possibilities.

The changes that we must react to and absorb can be wearing. McLuhan himself observed in a recent interview on the
mass society he describes that "I'm often supposed to approve

of these developments just because they're happening. I don't. I'm not very enthusiastic about any of these events. I find a certain pleasure in understanding them, but I would prefer a more stable environment, where nothing changes. You know, you don't want too many changes in one lifetime."[7] But, like it or not, the changes occur. Even as we have begun to absorb the implications of electric technology, we are being hurried forward into the new computerized age, in McLuhan's words "an age of the technological simulation of consciousness, when the creative process of knowing will be collectively and corporatively extended to the whole of human society, much as we have already extended our sense and nerves by the various media."[8]

It is, of course, in this third stage that the full implications of McLuhan as a "convergenist" are revealed. He is using every strong sensory impact, every type of advertising device, publishing gimmick, educational tool, to make us aware of the total, involved, multi-media, wrap-around experience that has become our lives. At this moment, according to Mc-Luhan, the past and the future are converging upon the present, and it is by focusing on the reality of the present moment instead of on the immobile and timeless essences once so largely the preoccupation of a culture which spatialized and visualized the message by means of print that we shall experience a growth in our interior resources great enough to encompass the growth in communications. Otherwise we are doomed to be inundated in technology and permanently paralyzed by the feelings of ennui that McLuhan mentioned he himself occasionally felt.

I've mentioned Teilhard and Lévi-Strauss in this attempt to encompass the historical-anthropological aspects of McLuhan's thinking. Teilhard saw evolution not as a biological matter but as an extension of man's senses and nerves through the development of his tools into an emergent and unforesee-

---

[7] *Ibid.*, p. 133.
[8] McLuhan, *Understanding Media*, pp. 3–4.

able future. Lévi-Strauss seems to have a somewhat more closed vision of man's future, for he sees the past as formative of the present and sees the future as a kaleidoscopic possibility developing out of the combinations and permutations of the breakdown of the present. McLuhan is not as rigorous a thinker as either, yet he intuitively seems to draw from both and be leading, if not to a new neolithic period or an Omega Point, at least to what Harvey Cox has called the Secular City.

Because we have the accumulation of knowledge about the past which we now enjoy, we can see the present as something distinctive, which both resembles and differs from the past in myriad ways. Self-study in terms of our past is an enterprise which no other age of man has been able to undertake, for it did not have the requisite kind of knowledge of its antiquity. This knowledge is growing in two directions: the further we get from the beginnings of our universe, the more we know about them; moreover, there seems to be an extrapolation of our knowledge of the past, through the present, into the future, so that our sense of presence now involves future ages as it hitherto never has done. Rather than being fearful of the new technology, we have reason to rejoice, for the convergence of past and future knowledge can be meaningful to the individual only through computerization and other electronic media. For individuals with adequate training, access to knowledge previously totally unfamiliar to them can be virtually instantaneous and total.

Rather than man's life becoming depersonalized by the machine and by mass culture, it is mass culture which is restructuring the psyche of every sensitive and informed person, giving man collectively a new sense of presence in and to the world. As McLuhan puts it:

> Electric circuitry did not create the public, it created the mass, meaning an environment of information that involved everybody in everybody. Now, to a man brought up in the environment of the public, the mass audience is a horror — it is a mess. In the same way, the public was a many-headed monster to a feudal aristocrat. He never bothered to study its structure any more than we study the mass. Circuitry brings people into relation with

each other in total involvement which creates the possibility
of dialogue and discovery on an enormous scale.[9]

There is actually a new interiorization of man's life as he is
confronted with a considerably greater scope of choices in action and in friends. He finds that he must expand his reflec-
tiveness to comprehend his new life. Thus personalist philosophers such as Gabriel Marcel and Martin Buber seem
quite as typical of our present century as our technology is.
Harvey Cox may suggest that we must work out an I-you relationship as a compromise between the reduction of the I-It
relationship and the exhaustion of the I-Thou relationship,
but even such thoughtful considerations register the intensity of the new psychological breakthrough. It is a breakthrough from the "world of sequence" into the electronic,
computerized "form of the icon" by accepting the "message
of the . . . medium."

McLuhan's theory of education and its concomitant psychology of learning also are connected with the phrases
"world of sequence" and "form of the icon" but it is the tag
line "The medium is the message" which is the core of his
thinking is this area. His most recent work, *The Medium Is
the Massage* (1967) is an explanation and illustration of his
views on education. It is a book nicely calculated for the post-
literate, non-book-reading age. It's not necessary to read *The
Medium Is The Massage*, for it is, as its subtitle has it, *An
Inventory of Effects*. You get the spirit of *The Medium* by
running your eyes over the illustrations, catching a word or
phrase here and there, permitting *The Massage* to produce
its effects even when it seems to be rubbing the wrong way.
And superficial though the contact may seem, McLuhan
maintains that we are being profoundly affected on a sub-
liminal level: "all media work us over completely. They are
so persuasive in their personal, political, esthetic, psychological, moral, ethical and social consequences that they leave

---

[9] McLuhan, "Address at Vision 65," *The American Scholar* (Spring, 1966),
p. 204.

no part of us untouched, unaffected, unaltered. The medium is the massage."[10]

The book really is a demonstration of McLuhan's ideas about total involvement in the educational experience. In his society of immediate communication, he wants simultaneously the fully realized individual functioning at his fullest in all directions, and an interacting mass, operating by intuition and instinct. He sees the college experience, for example, as moving away from instruction (in-struo, "pouring in") to real education (ex-duco, "leading out"). Thus, the recent phenomenon of the teach-in is actually a dialogue in which the audience becomes participant, in which the message is discovered or created by students and teachers working together in a charged environment. And thus in this book one really seems to be having a dialogue with the author. Open anywhere and flip forward or backward. Perhaps you'll come upon mirror type, upside-down pages, a cartoon from The New Yorker, a recorder voice print quiz. As McLuhan puts it, the book "is a look-around to see what's happening. It is a collide-oscope of inter-faced situations." "Happening" is the word. It is as close to a happening as a book can get: unpredictable, entertaining, vaguely discomfiting and unlysergically consciousness-expanding.

Indeed, on the matter of consciousness expansion, McLuhan mentions that he read a portion of Finnegans Wake to a young man, and at the end of the reading the young man said: "When you take LSD, the whole world takes on a multidimensional and multisensuous character of discovery. When I listened to Finnegans Wake I got the same experience as LSD."[11] "The Joyce expert, McLuhan, wants The Massage to be consciousness-expanding. Data-packed books have been filling a much-needed void in our new global tribe. This book, he hopes, will be "cool," will have less linear, logical matter and thus force us to "feel" the matter more,

---

[10] McLuhan, The Medium Is the Massage (New York: Random House, Inc., 1967), p. 12.
[11] "Address at Vision 65," op. cit., p. 205.

force us to become physically involved in a true educational experience. To achieve this type of impact McLuhan has tried to make the page "come-alive." He has explored and probed the typographical medium cinematically to move "into the world of creative configuration and structure"; he has played with and overlapped images, bled pictures over to the reverse of the page, used leaping continuity, changed the size and shape of sustained images from page to page.

But all this would be mere trickery if the pictures themselves weren't so frequently touching. They tell us something about the ultimate import of McLuhan's theories of which not even he seems fully aware. The tribal spirit which the selection of pictures conveys reminds me of Edward Steichen's lyric gathering of human faces and bodies and spirits in his great photographic exhibit in the Museum of Modern Art, *The Family of Man*. But though McLuhan provides memorable individual shots of striking faces and bodies, he would, I suspect, elect for showing them in the descending circularity of the Guggenheim and furnish roller skates for all. It might be dangerous, but it would be simultaneous and we would fill in the flashing spaces between the frames with our own visceral experience. Besides, McLuhan closes this typographical roller-coaster ride with A. N. Whitehead's observation that "It is the business of the future to be dangerous."

But McLuhan is doing more than offering an illustration of the Chinese proverb that a single picture is worth a thousand words. He is suggesting a modification in the psychology of learning to come to grips with a serious problem in our time. Robert Oppenheimer used to be fond of saying that "there are children playing in the street who could solve some of my top problems in physics, because they have modes of sensory perception that I have lost long ago." This is the same "integral being of the child" that Buckminster Fuller noted in the preceding chapter. And McLuhan shares this insight when he claims that "a child is a genius till he is five because all his senses are in active interrelation."[12] However,

---

[12] *Ibid.*, p. 203.

the genius is lost because, as the title of one of Paul Goodman's provocative works has it, the youngsters are *Growing Up Absurd*.

Education is a matter of the present, but we act as though we were caught between two worlds, one dead and one not yet born. As I have already pointed out, our age is unique in that it seems to be able to draw from past and future. Our educational system is absurd because we are already in that so-called not-yet-born age of the future, but we are behaving as if we were living only in the past. The children are more excruciatingly conscious of the absurdity than we are. As we move into the world of integral, computerized knowledge, mere classification becomes secondary and inadequate to the speeds with which data can now be processed. We are in the age of pattern recognition, out of the age of mere data classification. Children today live in a world in which the environment itself is made of electric information, but we adults attempt to make them live in our past. No wonder the communication barrier between those over and under thirty seems to grow more formidable every year. McLuhan maintains that we —

> . . . haven't really cottoned on to the fact that our children work furiously, processing data in an electrically structured information world; and when these children enter a classroom — elementary school — they encounter a situation that is very bewildering to them. The youngster today, stepping out of his nursery or TV environment, goes to school and enters a world where the information is scarce but is ordered and structured by fragmented, classified patterns, subjects, schedules. He is utterly bewildered because he comes out of this intricate and complex integral world of electric information and goes into this nineteenth-century world of classified information that still characterizes the educational establishment. The educational establishment is a nineteenth-century world of classified data much like any factory set up with its inventories and assembly lines. The young today are baffled because of this extraordinary gap between these two worlds.[13]

In education, then, "the medium is the message" and in our time that medium must not only be all-embracive it must also

---

[13] *Ibid.*, p. 198.

be "cool." McLuhan delights in using the word. It is part of the beatnik-hipster lingo and in its one syllable sums up a complex psycho-physiological syndrome. As McLuhan sees it, being "cool" rather than "hot" means being both aloof and involved — aloof from the particular, only to be more involved in the totality. It means being able to absorb the inevitable externalization of technology, while continuing to promote the harmonious internalization of human involvement. Being cool as an individual means being partly undefined, being flexible, being committed really to only one thing — education, your own education. "Growing Up Cool" is the real end — or I should say the means. Actually end and means get us as confused as medium and message, because growing up in a total way has become, in the age of electrically processed information, the major — and very difficult — work of everyone. But it is not difficult work really; in a fuller sense it is child's play. It is not an end; it is a role; it is a way of being; it is a lifetime of "be-in."

According to McLuhan the principal way the individual can attain and maintain coolness is by being immersed in "cool" media. The content is not really relevant. One can see a film in a theater or on TV. In the theater we have a "hot" medium since there is a high degree of definition. We sit back passively and ingest the material. It does not need our participation, only our appreciation. Of course films are becoming increasingly cool as movie-makers use fast-cutting, repetitions of frames, zoomar-lens takes etc. to force the viewer to work with the projector in assembling some sort of order out of the calculated dissociations on the screen. But take the "hottest" film of the thirties and send it over TV and it becomes cool. Instead of high definition we now see the image reduced to four hundred and fifty lines with spaces in between that we must imaginatively fill in. We are involved, we are participating. The medium in its cool way is only doing part of the work. Film is hot; television is cool. Books are hot; radio is cool. The cool medium or the cool person invites involvement.

And this whole issue of hot and cool media brings us again to the phenomenon of convergence in our time. McLuhan envisages a convergence of student and teacher, rather than a pouring of old ideas into fresh bottles. A lecture is hot since all the work is done. A seminar is cool provided everyone gets into the game. McLuhan prefers the total involvement of the teach-in which "represents a creative effort to switch the educational process to discovery, from package to proof. As the audience becomes participant, involved in the total electric drama, it can become a major work force; and the classroom, as much as any other place, can become a scene in which the audience can perform an enormous amount of work."[14] But the cool convergence goes beyond the classroom in the context of the cool media. By extending the seminar, the teach-in, to a mass audience through TV, computers, telephones etc., a problem — let us say one that had been bothering Robert Oppenheimer — could be presented to fifty million people. It seems inevitable that dozens of people in the participating audience would instantly see through any type of opaque problem. It would be extending "brain-storming" to a level which Teilhard would see as the noosphere itself in operation.

McLuhan's psychology of learning and convergence is not just a problem-exploring technique carried on by a cool group or a mass audience. This is but the external manifestation of an internal exploration which promises a much more profound convergence. McLuhan points out that —

> . . . if the unconscious has an important and irreplaceable function in human affairs, we had best look to it — it is being eroded at a furious pace; it is being invaded by dazzling investigations and insights; and we could quickly reach a stage in which we had no unconscious. This would be like dreaming awake. Such may well be the prophetic meaning of *Finnegans Wake*: his idea, among many others, that tribal man lived a dream and modern man is "back again Finnegan" into the cycle of the tribal involvement, but this time awake.[15]

14 *Ibid.*, p. 204.
15 *Ibid.*, p. 200.

This passage, suggesting that the unconscious is being made conscious, links McLuhan's theory of learning with his view of living history. History is seen as a process in time which is embodied — literally embodied — in me and you, as a dimension which you and I have, a dimension which in large part establishes our consciousness.

But this opening of the unconscious has palpable effects in the present. The cool are never frozen because they are constantly swimming from the waters of the conscious to those of the unconscious. Aldous Huxley, in his essay "The Education of an Amphibian," presents every human being as swimming in many different and incommensurable universes. Since that essay has much pertinence in our present discussion, let me quote at length:

> Every human being is a conscious self; but, below the threshold of consciousness, every human being is also a not-self — or, more precisely, he is five or six merging but clearly distinguishable not-selves. There is, first of all, the personal, home-made not-self — the not-self of habits and conditioned reflexes, the not-self of buried-alive reactions to remote events and forgotten words, the not-self of fossil infancy and the festering remains of a past that refuses to die. This personal not-self is that region of the subconscious with which psychiatry mainly deals. Next comes the not-self that used to be called the vegetative soul or the entelechy. This is the not-self in charge of the body — the not-self who, when we wish to walk, actually does the walking, the not-self that controls our breathing, our heartbeat, our glandular secretions. . . . Next, there is the not-self who inhabits the world from which we derive our insights and inspirations. This is the not-self who is responsible in all of us for every enhancement of wisdom, every sudden accession of vital or intellectual power. Beyond this world of inspiration lies the world of what Jung has called the Archetypes — those great shared symbols which stand for man's deepest tendencies, his perennial conflicts and ubiquitous problems. Next comes the world of visionary experience. . . . And finally, beyond all the rest, but immanent in every mental or material event, is that universal Not-Self, which men have called the Holy Spirit, the Atman-Brahman, the Clear Light, Suchness.[16]

The last three not-selves constitute the very essence of our being, but McLuhan avoids dealing with them. Perhaps the

---

[16] Aldous Huxley, "The Education of an Amphibian," *Tomorrow and Tomorrow and Tomorrow* (New York: Harper & Row, 1956), pp. 15–16.

Jesuits at Fordham University, where he has recently been appointed to the Albert Schweitzer Chair in the Humanities, will call his attention to this oversight. Under any circumstances I will reserve discussion of that spiritual recognition and convergence of being for the chapter on Norman O. Brown and Timothy Leary. Here I am interested in the convergence of the ego and the first three not-selves: the personal, the vegetative and the indwelling Spirit. McLuhan, too, I believe, is concerned with the healthy convergence of this quartet which is, on the temporal level, the psychophysical instrument by means of which we learn and live. Huxley maintains that "the disappointing results of education are due to improper use and loss of the natural standard of psycho-physical health. . . . We are so anxious to achieve some particular end that we never pay attention to the . . . means whereby that end is to be gained. . . . But the nature of the universe is such that ends can never justify means. On the contrary, the means always determine the end." And McLuhan, too, sees that the vegetative self becomes frozen if the child is forced to learn in order to gain approval, or if the college student must always keep his eye on the end, on the goal. Such freezing cuts off the intuitive moments that flow from the inner Spirit, the moments when the individual is in harmony with his environment and his inner being. As McLuhan puts it: "A child does not learn language as a series of meanings of words. He learns language as he learns to walk, or to hear, or to see. He learns language as a way of feeling and exploring his environment. Therefore, he is totally involved. He learns very fast because of this enormous sensuous involvement and the resulting motivation. It will be possible in this generation, I hope, to program the environment in such a way that we can learn a second language as we learned our mother tongue, rapidly and totally, as a means of perception and of discovery."[17] Perhaps McLuhan's whole psychology of learning is summed up in the approval he extends

---

[17] McLuhan, "Address at Vision 65," op. cit., p. 205.

to the young friend from Harvard who said: "You see, my generation does not have goals. We are not goal-oriented. We just want to know what is going on."

McLuhan's theory of art and sensory perception is closely related to his views of history and education. I mentioned in the opening pages of this chapter that art for him was identified with the future, but art also makes use of history's "world of sequence" and draws from the present as it attempts to educate us about modern media and their message. But McLuhan thinks of art at its most significant "as a DEW Line," a Distant Early Warning system that can always be relied on to tell the old culture what is beginning to happen to it. He believes Rimbaud, Joyce, Baudelaire offered just such signals when they ended "the era of literature as such" and founded literary modernism. All the latest artistic approaches such as "Theater of the Absurd," Camp Art, and Pop Art are characterized by their cool sensory treatment. All give us little surface data, provocatively hiding information to force us to involve ourselves more deeply in order to perceive their hidden depths and meanings. When McLuhan returned from a visit to Houston's new Astrodome stadium he was convinced that such structures were works of modern art which might well be the salvation of baseball, which as he sees it is much too linear, much too "hot" a game to really interest modern man. "But down there, under that roof, it's like being inside a pinball machine. The environment creates a whole new depth of involvement." The stadium, like Fuller's geodesic dome, provides a new medium, a new environment, that makes us see the game from a new and more personal focus. That, according to McLuhan, is essentially the artist's task. He does not have a message; he creates and/or reports-prophesizes a new environment.

As Susan Sontag tells us in *Against Interpretation*, "the model arts of our time are actually those with much less content than literature and a much cooler mode of moral judgment — like music, films, dance, architecture, painting, sculpture. The practice of these arts — all of which draw profusely,

naturally, and without embarrassment, upon science and technology — is the locus of the new sensibility."[18] They are
experimental probes. The basic unit for contemporary art is
not the message, but the analysis and extension of sensations.
Rilke described the artist as someone who works "toward an
extension of the regions of the individual senses"; McLuhan
calls artists "experts in sensory awareness." And the most interesting works of contemporary art are adventures in sensa-
tion, are "happenings," are "new sensory mixes." The artist
attempts to extend the viewer's sensibility by taking him out
of his environment, and by creating an anti- or counter-en-
vironment from which he can see the one he left. Only in
that way can the viewer become conscious of the rapid psychological, technological, and social changes that are taking
place. Flaubert said: "Style is a way of seeing." Conrad said
about the meaning of his work: "It is above all that you may
see." And Marshall McLuhan said:

> The training of perception upon the otherwise unheeded environ-
> ment became the basis of experimentation in what is called mod-
> ern art and poetry. The artist, instead of expressing himself in
> various patterns and packages of message, turned his senses and
> the work of art to the business of probing the environment. The
> symbolists, for example, broke up the old romantic landscape into
> fragments that they used as probes to explore the urban and
> metropolitan environments. Then they turned to probing the
> inner life of man with the same verbal instruments in hand. In-
> stead of using the verbal as a way of expression, they turned it
> inward for the purpose of exploring and discovering the contours
> of the inner life.[19]

Once again we see the converging of the exterior — the environment and the interior — the landscape of the mind. If,
however, convergence does not take place, conflict does, and
sometimes collision. Too frequently the landscape of the mind
is a rear-view mirror which has the individual living mentally
in an idealized pastoral scene while industrial and electronic
revolution continues around him. It is only the most cou-

---

[18] Susan Sontag, *Against Interpretation* (New York: Farrar, Straus &
Giroux, Inc., 1964), pp. 298–299.
[19] McLuhan, *The Medium Is the Massage*, p. 14.

rageous of the artists in any given era who "have the resources
and temerity to live in immediate contact with the environment of their age. . . . That is why they may seem to be ahead
of their time. . . . More timid people prefer to accept the
. . . previous environment's values as the continuing reality
of their time. Our natural bias is to accept the new gimmick
(automation, say) as a thing that can be accommodated in
the old ethical order."[20] In such instances we have the collision of cultures, for we are approaching the new with the
psychological conditioning and sensory responses of the old.
As McLuhan puts it: "In late medieval art . . . we saw the
fear of the new print technology expressed in the theme of
The Dance of Death. Today, similar fears are expressed in
the Theater of the Absurd. Both represent a common failure,
the attempt to do a job demanded by the new environment
with the tools of the old."[21] It is but an artistic variation on
Growing Up Absurd. Absurdity in the arts is, according to
McLuhan, a manifestation of the uncertainty and dis-ease
produced by our attempts to use the old forms which reflect
the old mechanical technology of classified data and of fragmented tasks to contain the new environment of integrated
knowledge. "The Theater of the Absurd dramatizes this recent dilemma of Western man, the man of action who appears not to be involved in the action."[22]

Before going further, I think I should make one considerable reservation about McLuhan on art. I think that his
analysis of the condition that produced the Theater and
the Art of the Absurd is valid, but I think he underestimates
the artist. The absurdists frequently are not frightened
but concerned or amused by our rapid advances, and they
are using their art to make us not only see the changes
but the absurdities involved in the changes. McLuhan seems
to have become rather "hot," become overly involved, in the
excitement of the new; and he displays consistently — perhaps

20 McLuhan, quoted by Sontag, op. cit., p. 299.
21 McLuhan, The Medium Is the Massage, p. 11.
22 McLuhan, Understanding Media (New York: McGraw-Hill, 1964), p. 5.

with calculation — an uncritical enthusiasm for all innova-
tion. Dramatists such as Ionesco or Pinter often dislocate the
real because it freshens the sense of reality. They often play
"against" the text: by grafting a serious formal production
onto a text that is absurd, wild, comic, or by treating a solemn
text in the spirit of buffoonery. But this does not mean a
failure of nerve, so much as a triumph of ironic cool that cannot be taken in. They are carrying McLuhan's theory of
cool just about as far as it can go. Not only is the medium
the message for Ionesco, but the message is meaningless.
What Ionesco did was to appropriate for the theater one
of the great technical discoveries of modern poetry: that all
language can be considered from the outside, as by a stranger.
Art for the absurdists is about nothing, but this message of
meaninglessness becomes a wonderful *massage*, a Rorschach
test, in which the audience participates, filling in the meaninglessness with a meaning of its own.

This, of course, is tantamount to saying that the absurdist
is "putting us on." He is! And he is doing it for the same
reasons that John Cage dares to have an audience listen to four
minutes and fifty-three seconds of silence while he sits before
his piano with an expectant audience out front staring at him.
In the silence we hear everything. Silence consists of all the
unintended noises of the environment. All the things that are
going on all the time in any environment, but things that were
never programmed or intended — that is silence. Silence is a
happening. One becomes tuned in to the medium, to the environment. You cough and you are the environment. Anal-
ogously in the theater of the absurd, if you think, if you
react, you are are the meaning since the absurdist has left
a void where the meaning should be. And the meaning
is the medium is the environment. You are in a counter-en-
vironment that permits you to understand your own changing
environment that much better. Such drama is not the product
of panic in the collision of worlds or cultures; it is the development of Chekhov's breaking string in *The Cherry Orchard*
that prompts both cast and audience to absorb the entire en-

vironment as they seek the cause of the totally meaningless, totally meaningful sound.

The trouble with modern theories of behaviorism, Hannah Arendt once wrote, is not that they are wrong but that they could become true. This applies also to McLuhan's theories of "Pop" and "Camp" art and their attraction for the mass audience. If he is right, then the old formal arts are no longer wholly meaningful and the artists are in imminent danger of being made redundant. For the impact of the "electronic culture" threatens to shatter all the traditional disciplines which were worked so hard for and acquired only slowly and with such difficulty. Pop Art and Camp must be read in part as do-it-yourself attempts to resolve the conflict between our pretensions to the finer things and our visceral adoration of the less fine. Pop, as a mode of expression, Camp as a shorthand style of appreciation, are both means of giving some sort of aesthetic-intellectual rationale to the fascinated attention we pay the mass media. It is probably a mistake on McLuhan's part to impute such depth to these movements, but as symptoms of a desire to move beyond the attitudes of cultural criticism as it is customarily practiced by literary people, they are indeed DEW lines.

They apparently do indicate where we are going. Pop clearly represents objects that have been rolled off a production line. They seem utterly without individuality, expendable, repeatable to infinity. They represent a depersonalized society. Yet in the depiction of tomato cans or Batmen, they do find a common denominator of appreciation and recognition. They are products of mass memory and mass production. And they are not, after all, so different from the Piscassos or Matisses mass-produced on plates and paper. The late works of Picasso certainly seem to me rather "pop" in that their spare lines and unsubtle colors can easily be reproduced on dinnerware. They haven't tried such methods on Rembrandt, I notice. Pop Art moves away from the past, moves away from pastoral scenes and mythic or religious subjects. It is a product of urban society and seems to be an extension or diminution of the interior decorator's art. Camp, on the other hand, is essentially the love of the unnatural: of artifice and exaggeration. They both share what Susan Sontag calls "the great discovery that the sensibility of high culture has no monopoly upon refinement. . . . The discovery of the good taste of bad taste can be very liberating. The man who insists on high and serious pleasures is depriving himself of pleasure; he continually restricts what he can enjoy."

Pop and Camp art are for McLuhan the "Revolt of the Masses" seen without the aristocratic disdain of José Ortega y Gasset. McLuhan sees them as helping to create a convergence in terms of common taste, a convergence which would be the product of the externalization of technology and the internalization of shared enthusiasms. He may be right, but, as indicated, I have reservations. When Teilhard uses the term convergence, he does not mean a lumpy pudding of common interest; he means a commune of uncommon interest and individuality united in love. McLuhan apparently has no inkling of the last three Not-Selves that Huxley mentioned in his essay on "The Education of an Amphibian," and consequently it is in this area of art where the world and its changing environments and the individual with his ego and not-selves meet in profoundest association that McLuhan seems untypically insensitive. Of course, we also have artists who have become so rapt with whatever is immediately at their nerve-ends that they have no time to attend to anything else or to respond at any depth. And such artists are rewarded with cash and publicity but these, I fear, are only consolation prizes for their not being taken seriously. They are rewarded not because they have real influence but because they have been relegated to a subdivision of the entertainment industry.

In spite of McLuhan's frequent awed references to James Joyce, I feel his theory of art contributes to this reduction of the artist. In his theory we have "the world of sequence" explained, "the message is the medium" demonstrated, but he does not give us "the inclusive form of the icon." His conception of the artistic icon excludes the personality, the uniqueness, the soul of the artist. I see McLuhan as a Voice of Convergence as he deals with history and education. I am disturbed by his theory of art. To paraphrase E. M. Forster, "Two Cheers for McLuhan."

CHAPTER IV

Enlightenment: Watts, Brown, and the Hippies

Incarnation is not to be understood carnally, for to be carnally-minded is death; that is to say, the body is not to be understood literally. Everything is symbolic, everything including the human body. To pass from the temple to the body is to perceive the body as the new temple, the true temple. The house is a woman; and the woman is a house or palace. . . . The land is a woman, the virgin land; and the woman is a land, my America, my Newfoundland. . . . Man makes himself, his own body, in the symbolic freedom of the imagination. "The Eternal Body of Man is the Imagination, that is, God Himself, the Divine Body, Jesus: we are his Members."
N. O. Brown, *Love's Body**

The unoccupied gulf between spiritual or brotherly love and sexual love corresponds to the cleft between spirit and matter, mind and body, so divided that our affections or our activities are assigned either to one or to the other. There is no continuum between the two, and the lack of any connection, any intervening spectrum, makes spiritual love insipid and sexual love brutal. To overstep the limits of brotherly love cannot, therefore, be understood as anything but an immediate swing to its opposite pole. Thus the subtle and wonderful gradations that lie between the two are almost entirely lost. In other words, the greater part of love is a relationship that we hardly allow, for love experienced only in its extreme forms is like buying a loaf of bread and being given only the two heels.
Alan W. Watts, *The Joyous Cosmology***

As a college teacher, I am particularly interested in the manifestations of "convergence" we are witnessing in today's youth. To understand this convergence, I have been reading Alan Watts, Norman O. Brown, and "underground" newspapers such as the San Francisco *Oracle* and New York's

* New York: Random House, 1966, pp. 224–226.
** New York: Pantheon Books, 1962, p. 93.

East Village Other, but most rewardingly I have been trying to read the youngsters, trying to tune in on them and get the message. I am in total disagreement with Karl Shapiro when he writes:

> I have seen what I think to be the ultimate generation, the generation of ultimate withdrawal. One sits around thinking of new names for them: The Autistic Generation, the Run-away Generation — what difference does it make? There is only one interesting thing about this generation: unlike all biological generational revolutions, this one does not want or intend to rejoin the human race, or so it argues. It rejects every stance which implies a discipline. In politics it cultivates amnesia, in poetics, aphasia. It adores violence and hysteria. It is the perfect cultural broth for fascism. The beat people had a marginal politick and a sense of community; their drug was weed. The new generation has no need of politick or community or poetry. They have acid.[1]

Shapiro's view is the most extreme of the eight presented in the *Nation's* teacher symposium on "The Class of '67" (June 19, 1967), but it is echoed in varying degrees in the statements of every one of the college teachers represented. Many of my colleagues, as well as the parents of college-age youngsters, seem to react just as negatively to the younger generation. When I protest, I am called "permissive." I've been told that much that is wrong with the college students today is the fault of people like me, who did not give them what they needed and really wanted — a clear image of authority.

I enjoy finding fault with the kids too; after all, the range of one's pleasures diminishes with the passing years. And fault-finding — faults in others, that is — can be very satisfying. But I believe the youngsters Shapiro so denigrates are the great hope of a promising convergence in our time — or in their time. To dismiss them is to reveal a serious hardening of attitudes and of arteries that will do nothing to diminish our own reputation as the Generation of Absurdity and Anxiety. The students do not intend "to rejoin the human race" as it is represented by our materialistic society. Many of them prefer to drop out and tune in on other philosophic and social approaches toward living the good life. Moreover,

---

[1] Karl Shapiro, "The Class of '67," *The Nation*, June 10, 1967, p. 777.

I suspect that there may be a political revolution brewing. Many of them would agree with Michael Novak (*Commonweal*, July 14, 1967):

> The new revolutionary mood is taking shape from a cauldron of evil, suffering, and pain. Enough young people have been beaten, jailed and even killed while trying to bring simple constitutional rights to American Negroes to have altered the inner life of a generation. The young do not think of law enforcement as the enforcement of justice; they have experienced it as the enforcement of injustice. . . . The policies of our nation must be altered. radically altered, not merely modified. . . . The logic of "realism" must be superseded by the logic of modesty abroad, social revolution at home, and a fundamental realignment of the bases of economic and political power in this land. 1976 must mark a revolution as important as that of 1776.[2]

The possibilities are there. Today fifty percent of the population is under twenty-five. No wonder politicians uneasily debate the pros and cons of permitting eighteen-year-olds to vote. As seasoned vote-getters they know they cannot trust anyone under thirty, since they do not represent anything youth stands for. They know there is a possibility of a third party — this one not based on economic or geographical lines but on the generation gap. If middle-aged movie-goers could make a governor out of such unlikely material as Ronald Reagan who knows what Alan Ginsberg might become if he can win the confidence of the S.D.S.

I am certain about my statistics and I am serious about my conjectures. This generation gap is quantitatively and qualitatively different from the traditional misunderstandings of father and son. And the revolutionary implications of that gap are almost as noticeable in Catholic universities as in secular ones. I was most interested in two articles that appeared in the *Catholic World* (January and July, 1967) based on two taped interviews, one with five students going to Fordham University, the other with six adults commenting on the students' comments. As the editor noted, "the six adults . . . did not quite come to grips with the precise issues posed by the five students." I think it would have been diffi-

---

[2] Michael Novak, in *Commonweal*, July 14, 1967, p. 443.

cult for the six adults to come to grips with such issues, for essentially there was but one issue: the youngsters did not want to become in ten or twenty years like the six adults.

Rather than indulging in the luxury of dismissing what we we do not understand, as did the teachers writing for the *Nation* or the *Catholic World*, we must try to bridge the gap. One reason I left Fordham for City College (a few years ago) was my dissatisfaction with my reactions to the students. I felt I knew them so well, knew their backgrounds, knew their religious questionings, because they were my background, my religious questionings. When I read such an interview, my first reaction was that an awful lot had happened at Catholic institutions such as Fordham in recent years. I reminded myself that Fordham's president, Father Leo McLaughlin, has gone on record as saying that he looks forward to student uprising at Fordham because it is better to discuss tensions than suppress them. In my years there my assumption that I knew all about my students seemed to me to be shared by my colleagues and the administration, an assumption that virtually prevented dialogue from taking place. I wonder if the six adults have dialogues with their students. It seemed to me they weren't even listening to each other.

I am sure that if Father McLauglin has had occasion to talk to Buell Gallagher, president of City College, he has been warned that one can get fed up with outspoken students. At City College I have no illusions about a shared background. I listen to the articulate and thoughtful, the sensitive and intense — say seven or eight percent of my students — and I listen to them as if they were colleagues. Or at least I try to. Frankly, I am the product of an unwind-your-tensions-on-the-class school of thought. As such there are times when I resent the young and their brashness. I resent having been a docile student complying with authority who, now that authority has been handed on to him, must face students who have little respect for his age or position. My authority is secure enough when the subject matter is pure literature, but pure literature is hard to come by. One has to say something about his reactions to a work and in doing so he can't help but reveal his position on God, sex, immortality, politics and goals in life, and that's where the dialogue begins.

In conferences that developed out of their remarks or my remarks in class, I've had heated discussions with students who were dropping out of college or who — though still getting good grades — were no longer interested in preparing to take their part in the establishment. I've gone down to the East Village, listened to their music, heard their justifications of pot and LSD. I've been to the Central Park Be-Ins. Still the following pages are only probes in attempting to define the dropout hippie situation. When I tried to sound a few of them out with the ideas I present here, they felt — predictably — that I was intellectualizing too much. I may also be projecting, and I may be idealizing.

Clark Kerr, former president of the University of California, dismisses the whole generation gap with its shifts in goals, gods, and politics as a promotional phenomenon: "Exaggeration is one word that fits. This new generation has exaggerated itself. It has been exaggerated and used, by the left and the right. It has been exaggerated by the mass media." He holds that underneath the exaggeration is a reality that goes back at least to Aristotle, who commented that young people "have exalted notions, because they have not yet been humbled by life or learned its necessary limitations. . . . All their mistakes are in the direction of doing things excessively and vehemently. They overdo everything — they love too much, hate too much, and the same with everything else."[3] Aristotle is right about the reality, and surely a teacher is right in counseling the "golden mean." But Kerr is wrong about the exaggeration. In our capitalistic society what better proof do we need of their influential numbers than the TV hucksters' imitations of their fashions and slang, or radio's omnipresent rock and roll, or the psychedelic floor displays

[3] Clark Kerr, "The Exaggerated Generation," *The New York Times Magazine*, June 4, 1967, 31, 36.

of Macy's and Gimbels? Or consider for a moment the phenomenon of Marshall McLuhan.

Kerr refers to the exaggeration of the mass media, but he does not realize that the medium is the message. In this case I use McLuhan's phrase to mean simply that it does not make any difference what the message about youth is. It is enough that the medium is preoccupied and preempted by youth. Their voices and sounds unite in a common electrical wave that inundates us with their presence. They have become a common age group and feel they have more in common with one another than with individuals within their own societies. One summer recently I visited London, Paris, Vienna, Athens and Rome, and whether it was the Spanish Steps or Piccadilly or the Left Bank the youngsters were united in an adventurous, poverty-enhanced sense of camaraderie that may have been reinforced by the mass media but which was realized in their actual contacts.

There is more to their unity than hair, beards, guitars and drug-and-sex kicks. There is more, too, than their ever increasing numbers. A good part of their sense of the group is linked with what McLuhan has called the electronic age. When I was growing up, even when I was in college, the old and those in positions of authority were likely to be venerated as repositories and bestowers of knowledge. In the past twenty years knowledge and techniques have changed so rapidly that many would-be educators realize that the finest thing they could do for the advancement of learning would be to remove themselves and make room for something that can be plugged in. We, of course, do not do so. No one likes to be yanked offstage before he has finished his act. But the young now want proof that what you have to say is relevant to this technological age. If they do not get it, some of them cool it; as you dodder your way through arcane demonstrations they listen with quiet tolerance and collect credits which will admit them to graduate school and a few more years' reprieve from the Vietnamese fiasco in which we are immersed. Others turn on, tune in, drop out.

It's the "others" I am interested in, and, given my position, I find it both ridiculous and agonizing to approve the "drop-out's" action. There is something amusingly repulsive about the middle-aged man with long hair, wearing sneakers, trying to be part of the Pepsi generation. I have seen these reconditioned instructorial squares figuratively rock and roll their way into general student disdain. Of course, all teachers who have much contact with students assume roles as brothers, uncles, fathers or grandfathers, depending on temperament and age. My own role has been fraternal and is now moving into avuncular. But the big brother in me has always and rightfully stepped aside for the teacher whose task it is to instruct the young in the complexity of the conditions on which the continuing life of society depends and in the limitations imposed upon the individual by emotional and social reality. Up to now I have been able to resist the seductions of rebelliousness for its own youthful sake, but for truth's sake I must admit that their spontaneous, communal and tolerant attitudes seem much healthier than the repressed, materialistic and bigoted positions of those who lead our society.

It is not enough to wiggle an admonitory index finger at these "hedonistic, sybaritic, self-centered, irresponsible, uncommitted kids." If we expect them to listen to our talk of a "golden mean," we must try to understand what is happening on the other side of that generation gap. We must tune in. Dialogue for the humanities is necessary. The sciences can demonstrate their relevance in our day, but the humanities must prove they are alive. To me the exciting and agonizing aspect of the modern drop-out situation is that, with understanding on both sides, the drop-out phenomenon could become a teach-in situation. They are carrying out of the classroom into life the very principles I teach. Prior to this I always had the uneasy feeling that, though my act was going over well, they knew that, given the present society, things taught in an English course must be unlearned after the degree has been awarded. Some of them have gone farther than I dared when I was a youngster, gone farther than I dare now, but my sympathy is with them. I wince when the hippie poet Gary Snyder declares that the revolution now being made by young people will leave not one value of the old America standing. I do not believe this, yet without considerable transformations in the American scene the values I think I stand for are meaningless. We of the older generation who consider ourselves sensitive and liberal cannot afford to drop out, but perhaps we can with their help distance ourselves a bit from smug, Christian, cutthroat, competitive compatibility, and perhaps in turn we can help them prevent their very real insight and force from drying up in the cold light of their early thirties.

The younger generation has both the practical leaders and the ideal goals necessary to motivate and activate a new political force. Activist or passivist, they are moved by disgust for much which our present society offers, and they repudiate many of its military, economic, and political demands. The student activists strident for civil rights and social and educational reform will be, in a few years, our politicians and administrators. They have the patience and stability for the drudgery of organizing and following through. They are as admirable as the college communists of the 1930's and ultimately will prove to be as futile, unless they are inspired to radical political reaction by their passivist contemporaries, the Zen-love-LSD-hippies.

There are the seeds of such a unity, I think. Katzman E. Bowart, the editor of The East Village Other, wrote in that underground publication in July, 1967, that "the most sophisticated method of the 'hippies' can be found in the newly formed Underground Press Syndicate. U.P.S. has almost fifty newspapers with a readership of close to a million. They speak essentially to their own people, but they provide a platform to counteract the establishment's control and unify a group of people who long before this phenomenon thought they were crazy. . . . The problem of becoming an institution, possessing collective power as a minority, before utopia can be accomplished can only be solved by our advanced tech-

nology, electronic and otherwise. . . . The hippies do point
to a solution, but that solution can only be solved technologically."[4] As Bowart sees it, the hippies are arrows pointing out the direction, but it will take others to draw the bow.
With a readership of a million there seems at least to be a
possibility. Certainly, in reading random copies of the San
Francisco Oracle and The East Village Other, I have been
frequently impressed by the intensity and quality of the
articles. These converging voices, naturally, are not always in
unison. Bowart's emphasis upon the technological suggests
that his vision has affinities with those of Buckminster Fuller
and Harvey Cox, but the Oracle seems to envisage a return to
the land. Both, however, are calling for a form of withdrawal
that amounts to a revolution.

What is so inspiring about the hippies, the dropouts? How
do their ideals, derived from disgust with the status quo,
echo mine drawn from literature? I can speak only of my own
"enlightenment." It was in the middle 1950's in Syracuse
University, where I was giving undergraduate courses and doing graduate work, that the revolutionary and radical implications of literature first struck me. This was the time of the
Eisenhower rest period, of the silent generation; but it was
also the time of the "beats." My students persuaded me to
cancel a class and attend a lecture given by Alan Watts, whose
name I vaguely associated with Zen Buddhism. The audi-
torium was filled with students. They were sitting on aisle
seats, perched on window ledges, everywhere. While the head
of the Department of Philosophy impatiently waited for the
students to settle down, Alan Watts leaned his head against
the back of his chair and seemed to relax. His mouth was
slightly open, his eyes moved about the room. He looked like
an academic, English Marlon Brando getting the feel of a
situation in his guts before emoting. The philosophy chairman finished his introduction and went back to his seat satisfied, having completed the slightly unpleasant chore of in-

---

[4] E. Boward Katzman, "Sgt. Pepper's Lonely Hearts Political Club and
Band," The East Village Other, July 1–15, 1967, p. 4.

troducing this popularizer of eastern cults. He settled himself down for a discreet afternoon's daydream. Watts stood up, strode to the lectern, looked about, lifted his hand in what seemed to be a greeting, slammed it down on the lectern, looked about once more and went back to his seat. That was the beginning of my "enlightenment." In that action I saw where literature and life converge, in that action the generation gap dissolved. The chairman, the representative of the establishment, was roused by the sound of one hand clapping. Discovering that Watts was again seated, he stood up and asked: "Are we to assume, Dr. Watts, that we have just heard your lecture?" The effect achieved, Watts returned to the lectern and explained that if that moment of sound, or the silence after the sound, could have been realized by the audience, there would be no need for him to say more.

Of course, it can be dismissed as a clever rhetorical trick, but for me the implications of that moment still reverberate. To be aware of the environment, to know that you are not an ego with a limited nervous system encapsuled in an envelope of skin, but an organic being united as everybody and everything else is with everybody and everything else around you; to be aware of the moment as a being free of domination, free of the Reality Principle, of the Death Wish, to be caught up in the Pleasure Principle, in the wish for a fully realized awareness, this is the true joy in life and is the ultimate message of poetry and great literature. And it is reflected in the youngsters' efforts to expand their consciousness, whether lysergically or not. They are experimenting with hallucinatory drugs, hypnotic dancing, strobe lights, yoga — to explore the moment in their own being, but they are also sharing that moment with others in their sexual adventures, in their experiments in communal living. Perhaps it is outrageous self-indulgence as our present society sees it, but then the youngsters see Vietnam and martinis as our self-indulgence. As their most famous button has it: "Make Love Not War." Moreover, I think you would have to go back to St. Francis or at least to the original dreams of the Catholic

Worker movement to equal the efforts of the "diggers," who are even left of the hippies, to run indigenous mission halls for the hippie brethren.

The diggers are anarchistic, communistic, and repudiate the present order by giving out free food, shelter, clothing and acid. They now have three farms outside the Haight-Ashbury district, growing and supplying food for the rest of the hippie community. And they do this without reference to money or production of goods and services or without intent of sapping allegiance from the people they serve. This past summer I was rubber-necking in Tompkins Square. A relatively presentable young man came up to me and asked for five dollars. I was embarrassed because this young product of our civilization was pan-handling, as well as confused by his request for so specific and large an amount of money. I used the usual lie, muttering something about having no money. He took out a quarter and attempted to give it to me with the remark: "You need it more than I do." We've got money and they need it, but they use it for various purposes, objective lessons in how futile the cash-nexus society is. Recall the much publicized incident on Wall Street in August, 1967, when a group of diggers threw dollar bills down on the clerks in the Wall Street Exchange, explaining after the chaos had subsided that they thought it was time the worshipers saw the color of their god.

This attitude was forcefully reflected in a symposium in San Francisco in which Alan Watts, Allen Ginsberg, Timothy Leary and Gary Snyder participated. All of them see our society at a crisis stage in terms of internal and external politics and economics. They believe that without a radical political and economic change, we will soon move into the horrors of 1984 and Brave New World. The symposium lasted for two hours, but the following exchange is representative of their views and those of the hippies:

> WATTS: But the thing is, that at the moment it is strongly indicated that all the values which are creating the disturbance, that is to say acquisitive values: that of buying things,

> possessing them, holding on to property, etc. etc. Suddenly
> this has become of no interest to the people who are really
> with it.
>
> GINSBERG: That's where the point of it is really; that there is
> an actual, empirical cultural change.
>
> SNYDER: The model of it is something like the Maha-Lila. . . .
> The Maha-Lila is a group of about three different families
> who have sort of pooled their resources, none of which are
> very great. But they have decided to play together and to
> work together and to take care of each other and that means
> all of them have ways of getting a small amount of bread,
> which they share. And other people contribute a little money
> when it comes in. And then they work together on creative
> projects. And they consider themselves a kind of extended
> family or clan. . . . The extended family leads to matrilineal
> descent and when we get matrilineal descent — then we'll
> have group marriage, and when we have group marriage we'll
> have the economy licked. Because with the group marriage
> capitalism is doomed and civilization goes out.
>
> LEARY: I foresee that these tribal groups that drop out will be
> helping to get back in harmony with the land. . . . They
> will be the tribal people, who won't have to worry about
> leisure because when you drop out then the real play-work
> begins.[5]

The tribal convergence that Watts, Ginsberg, Snyder and
Leary refer to, is, of course, not only a political matter, but
very much entails a radical view of sexual convergence, which
moves well beyond the conservative and essentially pessimistic
position of Sigmund Freud. I'm not suggesting that every
hippie has read Herbert Marcuse's *Eros and Civilization* or
Norman O. Brown's *Life Against Death*, but certainly the
four spokesmen mentioned above have, and a good number of
my students have been ardent enthusiasts of Norman O.
Brown.

Both Marcuse and Brown share the younger generation's
horror of the routinization of the imagination in the contemporary academy and in the world at large. They believe
profoundly that we must either change — and change in the
direction of total love — or else we must accept dissociation
from our environment and a personality permanently crippled

---

[5] "Symposium: Ginsberg, Leary, Snyder, Watts," *San Francisco Oracle*,
March, 1967, 30.

by repressions and enervated by fragmentation. They move from the Pelagianism of a willed political reform to the combination of a Pelagian willed-play and the modified Manichaeanism of an apocalyptic vision of the transformed body. It may be objected that Manichaeanism cannot be included in such a treatment of the modern generation, since the vision of Brown is of *Love's Body* and the delights and enlightenment proceeding not from liberation *from* the body but liberation *of* the body. However, in the following pages I expect to demonstrate that the Brown-Marcuse vision is one that transcends body in a timeless, all-embracing pantheism. To Marcuse and Brown true freedom can come only with the destruction of the mind-body dualism and a new, completely sensualized body in which eros or sexual love has moved beyond the genital zone, reconquered the whole body and extended itself in agape or universal love to all the contacts it makes in the world around it, turning the world into a paradise regained.

At first blush, such a view would suggest that these neo-Freudians should see a psychiatrist. However, they feel that anyone who sees a psychiatrist in our day should have his head examined. Marcuse and Brown feel that Freudian psychiatrists are committed to whatever society they find themselves in. If you are a capitalist, the psychiatrist will do the best he can to make you a reasonably adjusted capitalist. Only in this way can you pay his bills.

Recall that Gary Snyder in the San Francisco symposium spoke of the need for a matrilineal descent before the millenium could come. This is the very heart of the matter. The matter itself is a complex one, but in outline Marcuse and Brown hold that traditional psychologists are fixed on the father image, on the Oedipus story according to which we have a sense of guilt because of the primordial father figure whom we killed and because of the brother figures with whom we divided the kingdom. The super-ego in us is a cumulative, inherited state of consciousness which channels our sense of guilt, our death wish or reality principle, into socially useful projects. The pleasure principle or life wish of the individual is subordinated to what is useful for society. According to Freud, this pattern is an historically determined one and there is no chance of breaking it.

Marcuse holds that the sense of discipline, of order, of establishment which we experience at present is the major manifestation of this reality principle. To become liberated, we must experience a complete change of heart whereby work is not a disciplined activity, but is play in which we fulfill our own desires. Such "libidinal work relations are usually attributed to a general maternal attitude as the dominant trend of a culture. . . . Nature is taken, not as an object of domination and exploitation, but as a 'garden' which can grow while making human beings grow. It is the attitude that experiences man and nature as joined in a nonrepressive and still functioning order."[6] Thus the image of the mother replaces the image of the father. Self-fulfillment replaces competition and repression. The Law of Fidelity replaces the Law of Conformity.

Brown seems to go even farther. What we call reality or the reality principle, Brown calls illusion, lie, dream. We are asleep, and being asleep is being dead; we still live in the womb or return into the womb; our genital sexuality is regression to the state before birth; and we are still under the spell of the primal scene; we re-enact the father whom we have introjected; our sex life is his, not ours, and our pleasure remains vicarious. In Brown's most recent book, *Love's Body*, the Manichaean tendencies become rather obvious as he concludes that if all our life is dream and illusion, then the awakening to real life is the end of our life: death and resurrection are one. The way out of the womb, out of the dream cave, is to die in order to be reborn.

At this point Brown becomes mystical, moving into fire imagery and cosmic implications which are difficult to fol-

---

[6] Herbert Marcuse, *Eros and Civilization* (Boston: The Beacon Press, 1955), pp. 197–198.

low. His vision is one of Dionysian frenzy, Orphic rites and the no mind of Zen Buddhism, and he treats of them in dithyrambic iterations worthy of the most exalted gurus. He abandons logical and linear progression, organizing his sections loosely through the juxtaposition of relevant passages from diverse works, concluding with reflections of his own. His sentences or sentence fragments are often gasps, and whatever coherence and unity the "paragraphs" have is provided by the reader. He juggles words, distorts and rearranges the paragraphs, attempts to make the sense, the impact of a quotation come alive by involving the reader in the distortion and rearrangement. One thinks of McLuhan's medium messages and verbal massages and it is significant that he quotes that theorist so frequently in the work.

There is much in such disembodied nonlogical cosmic speculations which can be related to the hippies' views. But I will reserve that for later in the chapter when I touch on their drug-taking. There are also very significant points Brown makes in the two books. In the "Filthy Lucre" chapter, the central section of *Life Against Death*, Brown holds that the love of money as a means to the enjoyment of life is but the most obvious manifestation of the many forms of division, of inertia, of dis-ease, which plague our repressed society. He sees the concept of money, and the so-called rationality that conceived and maintains it, as a particularly dangerous form of "misplaced concreteness" whereby paper is hoarded rather than energy realized. It is the same "misplaced concreteness" David Bazelon attacks in *The Paper Economy*. In "Boundaries," which seems to me the central chapter of *Love's Body*, Brown quotes with approval William Blake's aphorism that "energy is the only life, and is from the Body. . . . Energy is Eternal Delight."[7] Both books constitute a plea and a warning that man must redirect his love, his overflow of energy, toward realizing that the self is but an extension of the other. Brown

[7] Norman O. Brown, *Love's Body* (New York: Random House, Inc., 1966), p. 161.

maintains that man is not historically neurotic, or at least only partially so, and that the individual has a deep-seated pleasure principle in him that can be released in a properly liberal environment:

> For two thousand years or more man has been subjected to a systematic effort to transform him into an ascetic animal. He remains a pleasure-seeking animal. Parental discipline, religious denunciation of bodily pleasure, and philosophic exaltation of the life of reason have all left man overtly docile, but secretly in his unconscious unconvinced, and therefore neurotic. Man remains unconvinced because in infancy he tasted the fruit of the tree of life, and knows that it is good, and never forgets.[8]

That childhood vision Freud refers to as polymorphous perversion. Brown and Marcuse prefer to call it pan-sexuality. Freud holds that the primordial garden of innocence can never be regained, although it is admittedly the secret goal of every man. The goal is not just the desire to find the oral, anal and genital areas all sexually satisfying — although it is that — the goal is to return to the original inability to distinguish between the so-called higher and lower functions and parts of the body. It is making child's play of work and taking with absolute seriousness Jesus' warning: "Unless you become as little children, you can in no wise enter the kingdom of heaven."

That's what the hippies are becoming — little children. It is totally irresponsible in the eyes of our Christian materialistic society, but they are playing at working a few hours a week — pan-handling, delivering mail, peddling underground newspapers, and working at play; that is, spending most of their time finding out who they are and opening up their sensibility, their consciousness, to the world and the people around them. William Hedgepeth, a *Look* assistant editor, lived as a hippie in the Haight-Ashbury section of San Francisco and wrote an article on his experiences. He closed his piece by quoting with approval a local cabdriver's observation that "The hippies are more honest with themselves than

---

[8] Brown, *Life Against Death* (Wesleyan University Press, 1959), p. 3.

anyone else is. Most people spent all their time working and enjoy life only as a sideline. With the hippies, life comes first, and work is the sideline."[9]

Of course, the idea of a dozen or so boys and girls sharing a pad is profoundly disturbing and secretly exciting to the sound and sensible members of my generation. Hedgepeth reports that, ironically enough, he was interviewed by a writer on contract to a confessional magazine and asked "questions too sexual and bizarre to repeat here. Within the limits of decency and accuracy and fantasy I 'confessed' to everything she suggested and everything I could think of — except that I was with *Look* — until she left, satisfied and smacking her lips."[10] But though this feature of the hippie adventure is played up, I don't think it is the most significant. We are all aware, at least through TV and *Playboy* and writers on contemporary mores, of the sexual revolution going on in our time. These youngsters, however, are not going to Third Avenue bars to find what weekend date the computer has selected for them. These youngsters seem to be taking individual sexuality and expanding it into more general areas. It is not simply a matter of bringing one's own genitals into contact with those of someone else. In breaking down the repressions and inhibitions, they allow the Pleasure Principle, eros, to flow through the whole of their lives and become agape, become flower power. In being spoken to, loved, and cared for, flowers and springs and animals and humans appear as what they are — beautiful, not only for those who address and regard them, but for themselves, objectively. Ideally, they are truly narcissistic; they have fallen in love with themselves, but they love their neighbor as themselves.

Such sexuality is a repudiation of the dominant father figure. It is a refusal to accept controls dictated by society and it is a reorientation to the original narcissism which engulfs the environment, integrating the narcissistic ego with

---

[9] William Hedgepeth, "Inside the Hippie Revolution," *Look*, August 22, 1967, 63.
[10] *Ibid.*

the objective world. According to Freud, the competition and antagonisms which characterize our present confrontation with reality are but a corruption of an earlier stage:

> Originally the ego includes everything, later it detaches from itself the external world. The ego-feeling we are aware of now is thus only a shrunken vestige of a far more extensive feeling — a feeling which embraced the universe and expressed an inseparable connection of the ego with the external world.[11]

And in being directed by one's own desires rather than being other-directed, work tends to become gratifying in itself without necessarily losing its work content. One is no longer alienated from the work, watching the clock, so that he can rush home from his living death to television and be video-goosed into buying something else that will force him to hire himself out to pay for it. The self-directed are capable of being lost in work because they choose it. They are like poets for whom time no longer exists as they search out their form and meaning. Poets have a love affair with the world. The same can be said of the hippies.

It is true that the world is not having a love affair with them, but they do not seem to be troubled. On the fifth day of the Newark racial riots last summer, Tompkins Square hippies brought flowers, candy, toothpaste, buttons and an oven to bake bread in right into the heart of the troubled area. It would be pleasant to report that as they sprinkled flowers, buttons and newspapers everywhere and as they rushed about mixing the flour for the bread, they were greeted with the same love they brought. Instead, the closed morality, the Law of Conformity prevailed. It was no surprise that the police arrested Jim Fouratt, one of the hippie leaders, because he was giving Negro kids piggyback rides. Besides, he refused to tell the police whether he was a boy or a girl. One is only thankful that the police did not club them for daring to bring the flowers and foodstuffs as the New York cops clubbed them in Tompkins Square for sing-

---

[11] Sigmund Freud, *Civilization and Its Discontents* (London: Hogarth Press, 1953), p. 120.

ing. (Three days later, the New York Times had a picture of angry property owners at Gracie Mansion violently pushing through a ring of docile policemen — this time no billies in sight — to present the mayor with their demands for higher rents.) But even the middle-class Negroes themselves identify with what the police are protecting. The hippies are bizarre, dirty, and obviously unsuccessful as our society understands success. One Negro mother said, "No child of mine would ever be hungry enough for me to let him get food that way." Another wanted the hippies to take their toys and get out. As she put it, "They are people who have nothing to offer this community. They don't have power to change things. They don't have any money to improve things in the slums. And from the look of them they can't even do much for themselves." Obviously it is hard to believe in or accept any form of love in our police-ridden, materially oriented society. This rejection of any spontaneous and outgoing action of love is symptomatic of the real social disease the hippies are fighting. But this and other such reactions are not justification for despair.

Recall once again Teilhard's radial energy or love that is the upward driving force of all on this planet. I'm not suggesting that Teilhard would have embraced the polymorphous perversions Norman O. Brown advocates in Life Against Death, nor would he be enthralled by Brown's espousal of tortured ecstatics from Dionysus to D. H. Lawrence. And yet Teilhard was profoundly conscious that worldwide charity and ultimate convergence could come only through encouraging that basic affinity of being with being, that drive toward synthesis, which has characterized the whole evolutionary process up to now. "The mutual attraction of the sexes is so fundamental a fact that any explanation of the world which does not succeed in incorporating it structurally as an essential part of its edifice, is virtually condemned."[12] And Teilhard moved beyond the traditional stand of the church when

---

[12] Pierre Teilhard de Chardin, "L'Evolution de la Chasteté," cited by Dan Sullivan in "Sex and the Person," Commonweal, July 22, 1966, p. 463.

he saw procreation as only one reason for sexual love and that reason, perhaps, not the most important. He writes in *L'Evolution de la Chasteté* that human love in its highest manifestation is an "attraction aimed at reciprocal sensitivizing and fulfillment, where the preoccupation with preserving the species is gradually being founded on the more profound rapture of creating, together, a World."[13]

This is not a chapter on Teilhard; yet his view parallels Brown on this sensitive issue so closely that one seems almost to be speaking for the other. If it be said that I have confused Teilhard's cosmic love, his agape, with Brown's body of love, his eros, I can only insist that the two men rejected the great line of demarcation between them. They were both opposed to boundaries. Indeed, there is an ecstasy in Teilhard when he writes of the physical attraction which becomes a spiritual attraction that breaks down all boundaries. The following passage from *The Phenomenon of Man* draws together the themes of convergence, eros and art, in phrasing and with a passion that is almost poetry itself:

> A sense of the universe, a sense of the *all*, the nostalgia which seizes us when confronted by nature, beauty, music — these seem to be an expectation and awareness of a Great Presence. The mystics and their commentators apart, how has psychology been able so consistently to ignore this fundamental vibration whose ring can be heard by every practised ear at the basis, or rather at the summit of every great emotion? Resonance to the All — the keynote of pure poetry and pure religion. . . . We are often inclined to think that we have exhausted the various natural forms of love with a man's love for his wife, his children, his friends and to a certain extent for his country. Yet precisely the most fundamental form of passion is missing from this list, the one which, under the pressure of an involuting universe, precipitates the elements one upon the other in the Whole — cosmic affinity and hence cosmic direction. A universal love is not only psychologically possible; it is the only complete and final way in which we are able to love.[14]

And Brown echoes this rhapsody as he sings of the human body which is "not a thing or substance" but "an energy

13 *Ibid.*
14 Teilhard de Chardin, *The Phenomenon of Man* (New York: Harper & Row, 1959), p. 266.

system." The boundaries must break down. Insanity, according to Brown, is the refusal to admit this unity, to attempt to repress it. Sanity rests in admitting that "every person . . . is many persons; a multitude made into one person; a corporate body; incorporated, a corporation."[15] Brown's "Garden of Delights" is composed of people whose doors of perception have been opened since they need no longer fear the death instinct, the instinct of aggression and division. Brown is not calling for disintegration, but for a breakdown of the old boundaries of ego so that a breakthrough into Utopia can take place. Seen from a certain perspective, there is nothing very new about it at all. It is as old at least as *Genesis*.

Our fall from grace is the record of our movement from animal instinct to awareness aware of itself. Now, in seeking our lost Eden, we must be aware of our thinking and loving the universe into continued being. Brown ends the chapter on boundaries with a paraphrased quotation from the New Testament: "He that findeth his own psyche shall lose it, and he that loseth his psyche for my sake shall find it." And Teilhard can ask in *The Phenomenon of Man*: "At what moment do lovers come into the most complete possession of themselves, if not when they say they are lost in each other?"[16]

If they are so in love with the world, why are the 15,000 or so youngsters in Haight-Asbury so determined to leave the world? It is one thing to drop out of the present society but they also drop out of the world they drop into. They use the lore of the East and/or drugs to escape the reality we all experience in common. It is in an understanding of the word "reality" that we come to an answer to this apparent paradox. Again I refer you to Freud's understanding of the Reality Principle and the Pleasure Principle. Freud writes:

> With the introduction of the reality principle one mode of thought activity was split off: it was kept free from reality-testing and remained subordinated to the pleasure principle alone. This is the act of phantasy-making, which begins already with the

---

[15] Brown, *Love's Body*, p. 147.
[16] Teilhard de Chardin, *The Phenomenon of Man*, p. 265.

game of children, and later, continued as day-dreaming, abandons its dependence on real objects.[17]

Moreover it is this phantasy or imagination which permits art, because it connects the unconscious flowing out of the pleasure principle with consciousness firmly committed to the Reality Principle. Suffice it to say at present that the dropouts are only doing what artists do. They are tuning in on their Pleasure Principle which is every bit as real as the world seen through the confining grid of the Reality Principle. Marcuse puts it well:

> As a fundamental, independent mental process, phantasy has a truth value of its own, which corresponds to an experience of its own — namely, the surmounting of the antagonistic human reality. Imagination envisions the reconciliation of the individual with the whole, of desire with realization, of happiness with reason. While this harmony has been removed into utopia by the established reality principle, phantasy insists that it must and can become real, that behind the illusion lies *knowledge*. The truths of imagination are first realized when phantasy itself takes form, when it creates a universe of perception and comprehension — a subjective and at the same time objective universe.[18]

Putting it in its extreme form, these members of the younger generation want to go completely out of their minds, for they realize that unless you lose your mind, you can't be sane. Unless — and I am here using Zen terms appropriated from books of Alan Watts — unless you break through "maya," the world of appearances imprinted in your psyche and fortified by every aspect of our society, you will never be able to attain "satori," or the enlightenment which permits you to see what a game this life is. Watts expresses that "enlightenment" eloquently, though somewhat unsyntactically, in the San Francisco symposium to which I referred earlier:

> Let's get back to a fundamental thing. I think that what you are really — all of you — having the courage to say, is that, the absolutely primary thing is that there be a change of conciousness in the individual . . . that he escape from the hallucina-

---

[17] Freud, *Collected Papers*, iv, p. 482.
[18] Marcuse, *op. cit.*, p. 130.

tion that he is a separate ego in an alien universe and that we
all come to realize, primarily, that each one of us is the whole
works. Each one of us is what is real and has been real for
always and always and always and will ever be. . . . That's what
you and I are, and we lose our anxieties and we lose our terror
of death, and our own unimportance. . . . That this is the
absolutely essential ingredient, which if we get hold of that
point, all the rest will be added unto you. . . . In the sense of
"Seek you first the kingdom of God and all these things shall
be added to you."[19]

Note that here as elsewhere Watts and the others charge
their message with a Christian aphorism which comes alive
in the alien context. This gives us a clue to the popularity of
Zen Buddhism. Certainly Zen is one way of going out of
your mind and attaining enlightenment, but it is effective in
part, at least, simply because of its novelty. The Buddha
sutra, the ragas, the mantrams, the images of Krishna, have
in our culture no negative associations, no sense of "old
fogeyism." And apparently the reverse is equally true. Watts
recounts that "in Buddhist churches in the Niseis (Japanese
American) they can't stand it when the priests chant the
sutras in Sino-Japanese language for the oldsters. They want
to hear 'Buddha loves me this I know, for the Sutra tells me
so.' They want to be as much as they can like Protestants
because that's exotic to them."

Though the exotic and bizarre may be intriguing, the
fundamental appeal is once again convergence. In *Psychotherapy East and West* Watts explores the relationship that
Hinduism and Buddhism have with the psychological knowledge of the modern West. He holds that the former "ways of
liberation have something in common with psychotherapy
beyond the interest in changing states of consciousness," for
both the psychologist and the oriental sage try "to help the
individual to be himself and to go it alone . . . to be in the
world but not of the world."[20] As Watts sees it, both East and
West in their theories of psychology and religion share three

---

[19] *San Francisco Oracle*, art. cit., p. 30..
[20] Alan W. Watts, *Psychotherapy East and West* (New York: Pantheon,
1961), p. 2.

converging avenues of enlightenment, though the West is limited because of its greatest success, i.e., rigorously exact physical knowledge. These three avenues can be seen clearly as Watts, in another of his works, *Nature, Man and Woman*, discusses that most basic of convergences, the coming together of man and woman. His point of reference is the East, but the religious and psychological insights are shared by sensitive western thinkers as well:

> It is true that in Taoism and Tantric Buddhism there are what appear to be techniques or "practices" of sexual relationship, but these are, like sacraments, the "outward and visible signs of an inward or spiritual grace." . . . Sexual yoga needs to be freed from a misunderstanding attached to all forms of yoga, of spiritual "practice" or "exercise," since these ill-chosen words suggest that yoga is a method for the progressive achievement of certain results — and that is exactly what it is not. Yoga means "union," that is, the realization of man's inner identity with Brahman or Tao, and strictly speaking this is not an end to which there are methods or means since it cannot be made an object of desire. . . . Yoga "practices" are therefore sacramental expressions or "celebrations" of this union, in rather the same sense that Catholics celebrate the Mass as an expression of Christ's "full, perfect, and *sufficient* sacrifice."
>
> Contemplative love has no specific aim; there is nothing particular that has to be made to happen. It is simply that a man and a woman are together exploring their spontaneous feeling — without any preconceived idea of what it ought to be, since the sphere of contemplation is not what should be but what *is*. In a world of clocks and schedules the one really important technical item is the provision of adequate time. Yet this is not so much clock time as psychological time, the attitude of letting things happen in their own time, and of an ungrasping and unhurrying interchange of the senses with their objects. In default of this attitude the greater part of sexual experience in our culture falls far short of its possibilities.[21]

Two of the converging avenues I have dealt with already. I have quoted at length because this passage is such an explicit statement about the sexual experience that can move from eros to agape. Even in the West no one has to be persuaded that coupling on the rear seat of a car is not as

---

[21] Watts, *Nature, Man and Woman* (New York: Pantheon, 1958), pp. 161, 165–166.

liberating as making love beside the ocean. The East goes further. There is the inner ocean of the unconscious that can be shared. There is a common "ocean" of being which if tapped makes the experience sacramental.

And this inner sacramental experience leads to the second avenue referred to previously. In moving beyond the corporeal sphere, we come to a form of cosmic consciousness; it is the shift from egocentric awareness to the feeling that one's identity is the whole field of the organism in its environment. This insight, too, is to be found in Christianity, but there is a peculiar active passivism about it as presented in eastern lore. When Watts speaks of "union," of "realization of man's inner identity with Brahman," he is not advocating mystic escapism. To the cosmic thinker, whether eastern or western, life is most fully lived when we do not live it, but when it lives us; when the ego is experienced as a cell in an organic whole. But this cosmic view is also active, for the cell realizes itself more fully by accepting the organic whole, by accepting the shared ocean. With this level of being we are in touch not with "reason" but with that force from which, as Aldous Huxley expresses it, flows "every enhancement of wisdom, every sudden accession of vital or intellectual power; in it we find confirmation for Archetypes—those great shared symbols which stand for man's deepest tendencies; it is the universal Not-Self, which men have called the Holy Spirit, have called Atman-Brahman." For some, to listen to the repetitions of a litany or the involved variations of a raga is to experience the melting of self into the Not-Self. This is not an escape from the world; it is an immeasureable enhancement of the world.

I am not taking my readings in Alan Watts, Aldous Huxley, and William James and arbitrarily imposing them on the hippies. Their enthusiasm for and knowledge of eastern lore seems to be really quite significant. For example, the question of cosmic consciousness and the convergence of East and West is dealt with quite masterfully in an unsigned article, "The Advent of the World-Teacher" in the March

1967 *Oracle*. (I might mention in passing that this underground newspaper is obviously a labor — or a play — of love. The articles really do tune one in on what is going on among the Hippies and the artwork and typography, though sometimes confusing to middle-aged eyes, is delightfully like that of William Blake in its attempt to bleed color and form into the text.) The article quotes a section of the *Bhagavad Gita* called "The Collabria" and comments:

> What does Collabria mean? We'll have to talk all around the question to make it clear, since all terms are semantic limitations, both revealing and concealing meanings. If the terms God, Brahman, the Buddha, nature and so on were all understood in their broadest senses, we would have no new terms for cosmic realities. . . .
>
> Teilhard de Chardin comes perhaps closest to Collabria with his term, Noosphere: a humanized energy belt which has charged the world, bringing it ever closer to total enlightenment and the completion of its destiny.[22]

The third avenue of convergence deals with time. Watts speaks of psychological time rather than clock time. This is roughly equivalent to Henri Bergson's distinction between duration and chronological time, that is, the knowing and living soul is involved not with the ticking but the experience. Of course, in every one of these approaches it is maya, appearance, the grid, that is being overcome. Here it is the illusion of measured time and the necessity of a programed day that is being questioned. Certainly the fact of mortal mutability cannot be questioned, but we in the West are often caught in a bind. Since all things change, what is the purpose of striving for anything? The death wish takes over in a subtle way as we rationalize a wasted life with the thought that death is not far away. This was the problem Shaw wrestled with in *Back to Methusalah*. Or if we accept the consolation of the promised eternity, that too only emphasizes the mutability of earthly things. What sense is there in enjoying the here when eternity on a superterrestrial level awaits us?

---

[22] *San Francisco Oracle*, "The Advent of the World Teacher," March, 1967, p. 35.

But to capture the moment out of time is to experience its "thisness." You and the object are one, and your fulfillment is in being the object and the object being you. Certainly in doing this one springs to the cosmic level already mentioned, but first it is necessary to immerse oneself in the very object before one. It is necessary to believe in the object as it is in itself. As Marcuse puts it: "Man comes to himself only when . . . eternity has become present in the here and now."[23] Such meditation in time that takes you out of time is not so different from the three stages of meditation recommended by Ignatius Loyola. To attain a proper attitude toward a biblical event, Loyola first recommended a mental representation of the scene; e.g., evoking imaginatively every detail of the birth of Christ. One could, of course, use a physical reconstruction such as a crèche to facilitate this stage. Second, one projected himself into that scene, into that time, perhaps becoming a shepherd. Finally, the moment of colloquy might occur in which the scene, now out of its historical time and out of your ticking time, spoke its eternal truth to you alone.

All of this begins to be a bit heavy as I present it discursively. But the existential happening itself is profoundly simple. To sum it up, Watts, using the religions of the East — but aware that Christianity in an uncluttered state makes the same points — recommends that the wise man jump out of his skin, go out of his mind, and drop out of time. Enlightenment, then, is equated with total liberation, and that means liberation from cause and effect, liberation from meaning. There are hundreds of stories illustrating that the basic position of the Zen master is to have no position, nothing to teach, no doctrine, no method, no attainment or insight of any kind. One of my favorites is that of the Zen student coming to the master and asking how he should attain satori. The master answers "Eat your rice." The student says he has done so. The Master responds: "Then wash your bowl." The point being, if one can talk about points, that satori is in the moment, any moment that is realized. But such realization

---

[23] Marcuse, op. cit., p. 15.

is not easy. The seeker cannot concentrate his reason upon the problem, for the lack of reason and will is a part of the attainment; he must somehow exercise the will power of desirelessness.

The hippies are searching for that "enlightenment" of which Watts writes. They are seeking it in eastern lore and practices, in sexual freedom, and in the use of drugs, particularly LSD. In this area, too, Watts is a perceptive commentator. In 1962 Watts took LSD for the first time and wrote a book, *The Joyous Cosmology*, in which he confessed that "I am . . . at once gratified and embarrassed by this development in Western science which could possibly put the unitive vision of the world, by almost shockingly easy means, within the reach of many who have thus far sought it in vain by traditional methods."[24]

Watts found that the fundamental insights he experienced when he took LSD were the same as the three characteristics of Taoism and Zen Buddhism he had described in a dozen books: Timelessness, Unity, and Love. With dithyrambic iteration in *The Joyous Cosmology*, he sings of the LSD world which "has a kind of time. It is the time of biological rhythm, not of the clock and all that goes with the clock. . . . I am not looking *at* the world, not confronting it; I am knowing it by a continuous process of transforming it into myself. . . . I became curiously affectionate and intimate with all that seemed alien. At root, there is simply no way of separating self from other, self-love from other-love."[25] That Watts would equate the "satori" or enlightenment achieved through the rigorous discipline of Zen with these chemically induced reactions seemed to me at the time like outrageous charlatanism.

Two years later I took lysergic acid myself and the vistas opened to me redeemed my confidence in Watts. I found myself resorting to my own disciplines to describe those

---

[24] Watts, *The Joyous Cosmology* (New York: Random House, Inc., 1962), p. 12.

[25] *Ibid.*, pp. 27, 29.

vistas. They were within the range recorded by the romantic poets, particularly Blake, as well as by Gerard Manley Hopkins, William Butler Yeats and such archetypal novelists as Herman Hesse and George Macdonald. I recall in the flush of my first enthusiasm startling the sedate New York Shakespeare Club with a lecture on "*The Tempest* and LSD." (The president of the group confided afterwards that by LSD she thought I was referring to Shakespeare's box office appeal: LSD = Pounds, Shillings, Pence.) I took the drug only once: it has since, as everybody knows, become illegal even in medical practice. Moreover, it now seems "highly probable" that continued use of LSD can cause damage to chromosomes in all the cells, including the sperm and ovary cells.

Be that as it may, since I am not a creative artist or mystic, since my training, my imprinting, if you will, was so non-sensorially oriented, was instead so Jesuitically and analytically directed, it was at only infrequent moments that I experienced anything like the cosmic selflessness that is the basis of art and is the ultimate truth of life. Oh, I was able to appreciate a good poem and intellectually organize that appreciation, but now I know with some sense of exactness how confined I was and am; I have empirical knowledge of the artistic, perhaps even of the mystic, and I find my consciousness attempting to expand — unlysergically these years — to comprehend areas that once I did not even know existed. The lysergic acid experience is, I discover, the acid test. The drug does not miraculously change you or the world; it merely heightens and intensifies. If you are a horror or a fool, you will see a horrible or foolish world. Watts' acid world was a timeless, ego-less, loving Zen world, mine was pantheistic with literary and Catholic tendencies. We continued to wear the same old spectacles, but these now could become disconcertingly, alternately and sometimes simultaneously telescopes and microscopes.

I am actually a rather cautious academic type, and this kind of public confession of having seen the "true light" does not go well with me. Even the thought of being classified as one of "the true believers" with maniacal enthusiasm for questionable causes embarrasses me almost to the point of wanting to stop writing. Almost! You will have to read the following paragraphs with the understanding that I am not proselytizing for the indiscriminate use of what I know to be a potentially dangerous drug, but exploring an enlightenment I had and perhaps explaining one aspect of the generation-gap syndrome.

These days I am also embarrassed by the other Dr. Leary appearing in guru costume with weird necklaces, long hair and show business techniques, preaching his LSD sermons to teeny-boppers who have yet to experience their consciousness unexpanded. In his League for Spiritual Discovery (LSD) Celebrations down in the Village, Leary has reduced himself to what one hippie called an Aimee Semple McPherson in drag, or what I saw him to be — a false prophet irresponsibly blathering children into serious brain damage, when he might have been an avenue — as William James before him — for the serious consideration of other modes of consciousness by those who feel they have exhausted the present one. My stand probably seems contradictory. Not so. I am advising "tuning in" and applying the "golden mean." Let me explain.

Three years ago I attended a cocktail party given by a publishing house. When I was introduced to one group as Dr. Leary, one very attractive young lady was galvanized into attention and asked me if I was the Dr. Leary. I told her she was mistaking me for Louis Leary, the chairman of Columbia's English department. Using tones that coldly drew the square around me she made it clear she was not thinking of Louis but of Timothy. Shifting my martini and approach, I hastened to assure her that I had heard Leary and Alpert on WBAI and was immensely interested in the whole LSD question. But it was not to be. I had lost her interest. She soon wandered elsewhere, looking, I presume, for sugar cubes.

However, there had been a psychiatrist and his wife in the circle. A bit later he asked me if I was interested enough in LSD to consider taking it. He explained that he was conducting experiments with the purpose of discovering the drug's effect on reasonably bright and articulate people. We went out to dinner and continued the discussion. When I was assured that he and his wife had taken it twice with no ill effects, I tentatively agreed. One week later I went to his home and met his wife once again and three other "reasonably bright and articulate people": one man, an artist; and two women, a nurse and a college teacher. In the meantime I'd had a chance to check out the psychiatrist's reputation and found him to be well-known with a number of books to his credit. On that evening and on one additional meeting the following week, we sat in his library, sipping drinks and talking. He assured us that though a tape recorder was going during all our sessions, he would use nothing in a book he was planning without our permission. Our identities, of course, would not be revealed. These meetings gave him a chance to be reasonably certain that we were not seriously neurotic and it gave us a chance to sound out our reasons for taking the drug.

I was by no means certain that I wanted to take LSD. I share with most intellectuals in our age a dread of becoming a thing, of being even further manipulated. Viewed from one perspective, the use of LSD was an admission of defeat. It seemed to me a confession that since I couldn't regulate the outside world, since I couldn't modify the stubborn, irreducible facts outside me, I was modifying my inner being artificially and blocking out reality with illusion. Moreover, I knew that even though I was only taking a relatively modest quantity of 250 micrograms of LSD, there would be at least three hours of the eight-hour trip when I would only be in partial control of myself. For a person brought up to keep himself under tight rational control with the exception of social drinking this was particularly disturbing. Of the internal horrors that might rise from the deep I was only mildly concerned, since I was assured that the session would be so directed that most of my stimuli would be external. Moreover there was a thorazine shot that could be given if repressed memories released in a tremendously augmented sense spectrum proved overwhelming.

However, my reasons for taking LSD at that time bore even more weight with me. I had read Aldous Huxley's *The Doors of Perception* and William James' *Varieties of Religious Experience* some years before. Watts' *The Joyous Cosmology* I reread that week. I had and have considerable respect for their brilliant, searching minds. I had taken a forced march with Aristotle and Aquinas during most of my life; why not demonstrate fidelity to the curiosity, intuition and avenues of perception that still so intrigued me? I was dissatisfied with what I saw of the world. I knew myself to be a disciplined individual never unduly influenced by my environment. Rain or shine, rural or urban, my environment both visual and mental, was always a clean, well-lighted, little place. I had come to the middle of my journey and I wanted to see if I could become lost in the woods. Moreover, a number of my students confided to me that they had taken LSD. They were inarticulate but ecstatic. I could sense even then that the generation gap that was already making communications with my students difficult would be immeasurably widened between those who had this experience and those who did not. Finally, it seemed awfully "chicken" of me to give up such a ready-made controlled situation. I knew I could probably take the drug at another time, but that I would never have a better and safer opportunity.

The afternoon of the trip arrived. I had been advised to bring works of art that I felt comfortable with and would like to understand better. I brought a recording of Beethoven's Fourth Piano Concerto played by Arthur Schnabel and three prints by Picasso, Cezanne, and William Blake. I also asked the psychiatrist and his wife, who were guiding our tour and not taking the drug themselves, to read me selections from the poems of Blake, Eliot, and Hopkins when I was "high."

We were once again in the familiar, orderly and cozy library. We continued our conversations. There were two differences. There was a beautiful bouquet of spring flowers on one table near us and instead of gin in my tonic I had lysergic acid.

For a little less than an hour I continued conversation and then I lost contact with everyone in the room but our guides. It was an exhausting session and I find it difficult to believe anyone would desire the experience on a weekly or monthly basis. But in its initial impact and in the last analysis it was the most exciting, fulfilling body-mind experience I ever had.

One sentence of T. S. Eliot's that shook me during the trip is vital in understanding the importance of the experience. Eliot writes in *Four Quartets*: "We had the experience but missed the meaning,/ And approach to the meaning restores the experience/ In a different form, beyond any meaning/ We can assign to happiness." Eliot is coming to terms with moments in his own life when the veil of consciousness trembled and gave intimations of other possibilities. He speaks of what I know. And in my knowledge I accept that truth but I find that the reverse is equally true: "I thought I knew the meaning but I missed the experience and a turning to the experience confirmed and augmented the meaning in a wider and deeper form." The taking of LSD for me and others I have talked to seemed to draw a line under the column of my years and permitted me to add them up. What I was — or at least what was permitted to emerge in the tranquil, warm atmosphere of that library and that group — revealed itself to me, and I knew with Dame Julian that "all shall be well and all shall be well, and all manner of thing shall be well." What I knew was what Watts had known: the profound reality to be found in losing one's identity, merging one's mind with the universe and transcending time.

Did I have a mystical experience in the psychiatrist's library that spring afternoon? I still have no answer to that question. It is reassuring, though, to find that this very question of mysticism and LSD has had prominent coverage in the

London *Times*. The whole issue was treated with such candid sanity, I cannot help but quote at length. In a leading article (July 15, 1967) the unidentified writer refers to the ecstasy experienced through hallucinogenic drugs, but observes that "this ecstatic feeling is not, as some people have supposed, the core of the mystical experience, which is something much rarer and undoubtedly much higher. Yet ecstasy is the religious experience which has commonly been a prologue to the development of the mystical life. It is also in empirical judgment the strongest single argument for the existence of God; according to this argument God is believed to exist because so many millions of mankind, at all times and in all places, have had an experience of the divine." And he concludes with a wise warning and a useful distinction: "In order to operate normally, man needs to be insulated from the divine wind that blows through the universe, just as he is insulated from cosmic radiation by the earth's atmosphere. He seems to have a mental shield which protects him from a sense of the immanence of God, just as his bony skull protects the pulp of his brain. In some people this skull of protection is so thick that no sense of mystery can ever enter and some minds are further protected by the world's materialism. Certain powerful influences, religion, contemplation, green fields, madness and drugs, which operate on the biochemistry of the mind, can fracture the protection and expose the human mind to a divine experience. The experience is one which only humility and spiritual wisdom can properly contain or comprehend. For the young and inexperienced the psychedelic drugs are a type of conjuring with superior power which must be dangerous and wrong, and the more powerful their effect, the more dangerous they must be."

By July 25, 1967 the *Times* had published twelve letters responding to this article. Perhaps the letter of Mr. Christopher Mayhew, Labour M.P. for Woolwich, East, puts the positive side best. He reports: "In 1955, acting as a guinea-pig for a well-known psychiatrist, Dr. Humphrey Osmond, I took an LSD-type hallucinogenic drug and had what was

even then called a 'psychedelic experience.' . . . Part of my
motive was to test a theory in my book *Men Seeking God*
. . . that there is no clear dividing line between mystical experiences induced by sanctity, mental sickness and hallucinogenic drugs." His conclusion seemed to be "that a great controversy will in due course develop between the 'thick skulls'
. . . and the 'thin skulls.' At the moment the 'thick skulls'
hold the field, and their case is greatly strengthened by the
antics of 'hippies' and by our dangerous ignorance of the
crude drugs now available; but there is a fascinating case
waiting to be developed on the other side, challenging almost
all the beliefs and values of contemporary society."

Did I have a mystical experience? I don't think so. I hope
not. I don't like the idea of instant satori any better now than
when I first read Watts book. I do know that my senses
opened and all of them seemed to be interconnected. I experienced the synaesthesia I had lectured about in teaching
Rimbaud, Baudelaire, and Gerard Manley Hopkins. That is,
colors and sounds seemed to become each other. As I looked
at Picasso his reds became palpable and tasted, well — tasted
like watermelon. The deep blue of a drape that had been
stirred by a breeze coming through the window permeated the
entire room. If I had been creative, I would have wanted to
capture that drape's blueness and merge it with the silver of
Beethoven's Fourth Piano Concerto. That concerto was "vis-
ually" like a Disney psychedelic *Fantasia* without the work
freezing into a static pattern. (I still can't hear Beethoven's
"Pastoral" without seeing Disney's little horses.) Heard notes
became — it seemed literally — silver globes that continued to
sound in some delayed memory sense while the continuing
themes were superimposed upon these hovering patches of
sound. I have a friend who says you must have three ears to
appreciate Bach. That afternoon all my senses were multiplied
by six and linear time had dissolved so that in the end of the
work was its beginning. I heard both simultaneously.

I knew I could never equal Beethoven or Cezanne, but
in my expanded powers of appreciation I was Beethoven and

Cezanne and their work combined "creatively" in my mind.
I knew that no amount of LSD was going to make me into
a Hopkins, but I could understand the excitement of his
"Nothing is So Beautiful as Spring" sonnet as I experienced
the colors, the music, the tastes, the whirl of the room and
the whirl of my memories around the bouquet of flowers on
the table. It seemed as though all my reactions and memories
were pulled out by even one of them being plucked from the
tightly-packed neural patterns of my brain.

But oxymoron or lyric contradictions can hardly convey
the experience. When I heard the playback, the contrast
between my remembered joyous experience and the visceral
grunts and mumbled recordings was laughable. I had Fuller's
and Brown's "integral being of the child" together with the
unblocked sensibility of William Blake. But even these
retrospective effusions are little help in expressing the experience. Again T. S. Eliot: "And so each venture/ Is a
new beginning, a raid on the inarticulate/ With shabby
equipment always deteriorating/ In the general mess of
imprecision of feeling,/ Undisciplined squads of emotion."
From my own experience and from talking to the other par-
ticipants, I gather that the complexity, the imprecision, the
mess, are always a part of the trip. Timothy Leary is wrong
when he lectures about the psychedelic terrain for which he
is able to prepare maps. The context we play our sensibilities
and memories against may well be the same, but we bring
ourselves into that terrain and the experience is largely what
we are, though magnified and unbounded. The effect is
schizophrenic in that your familiar but amplified ego is still
there but somehow you are also the context against which
the ego is playing. You are creator and creature but the two
aspects of creation affect one another and the experience is
confusing, even disturbing, and can be terrifying. Watts,
speculating about LSD in *Nature, Man and Woman*, con-
trasts the drug's effects with that of the mystical experience
and concludes that "The drug gives a vision of nature which
is infinitely complex, the mystical state is clarifying, and

gives a vision which is as infinitely simple. The drug seems to give the intelligence a kaleidoscopic quality which 'patterns' the perception of relations in accordance with its own peculiar structure."

I came with a certain background into the experience, and this background was not only sustained but heightened. I also know youngsters whose range of interests and intensity of reaction have been appreciably expanded after use of the drug. However, I've also been to underground movies made by teams of young directors who employ a wide range of electronic gadgets to convey the experience as they knew it. One I went to a few months ago utilized half a dozen film and slide projectors, variations of lumia, diffraction hexes, oscilloscopes, strobe lights, several sound channels and all of this was assembled to project simultaneously various phases of an interminable motorcycle ride and an incredibly long orgasm. And so finally the school teacher in me is revealed. Those whose sole interests are motorcycle rides and sex have no need of consciousness expanders. There has to be a certain number of pieces in the mental kaleidoscope before stirring produces positive effects. As Lear's Fool puts it "Nothing comes of nothing."

There is, however, something other than one's own peculiar personality involved in the LSD trip. The sum total of one's own experience determines how that other will be viewed and whether it will be a good or bad trip. Paul Tillich writes of the "ground" of being which is God. I felt that I was part of that "ground," that my will was God's will in that I willed nothing. I was outside of time. When I looked at my own hand or at the face of the psychiatrist or at the bouquet of flowers, I did not see aging skin, lines and mutability. I saw what Hopkins saw: "There lives the dearest freshness, deep down things." The moment and the object sufficed because I was realizing the external object at any moment. At any moment I *was* that object. Subject and object were one. Again, I had read about such matters, talked about them, had the audacity to lecture about them, but for a time I knew viscerally what the mystics, the romantic poets, what Alfred North Whitehead and the modern physicists, what James, Huxley and Watts had meant by enlightenment, or prehensive unity, or the still point.

Everyone on that trip had felt this organic merging of the self with universe. Afterwards, in listening to sections of the other tapes, I realized that this was the crucial experience and test. The senses trick us and the "normal" view of the world is every bit as much a trick as the phantasmagoria we witnessed that afternoon. But the limitless drop into oneself was real. We had been warned of this moment and told to "roll with it." One of us didn't. The artist tried to hold on and he was in agony as all he knew himself to be seemed to flow out of him while he tried to retain his identity. Apparently the thorazine was used, for abruptly his pain subsided. He told us afterwards that he would never take LSD again because he found it profoundly disturbing to conceive of a God who was not out there but in here, in our own being, and as an artist he had a conception of order that would be completely destroyed if he accepted the dissolving boundaries he seemed to have experienced. His objections were valid, and apparently his instincts were sound, for he has gone on to become a rather well-known artist. Still those very objections were for me the source of inspiring affirmations.

The organic merging I felt was the ultimate convergence, the convergence of the pleasure principle and the reality principle, of life and death. Putting it simply, I was totally gratified by all that I sensed around me. I was identified with it in a perception that was a consummation. At the same time I accepted the limits. I thought of the possibility of death in my fall into myself, in my "night journey," but this too I seemed to be able to embrace in my will. My ego was still there, but its little whining voice was silent. One of our reasons for fearing death — unless, of course, we have been trained to fear hell — is that we want to be or do something more. I could not want anything because I had everything. That ultimate convergence has been movingly presented in an article by Sidney Cohen, M.D., "LSD and the Anguish of Dying" (*Harper's Magazine*, Sept. 1965) in which Doctor Cohen presents the tape recorded comments of a nurse dying of cancer. She had been given LSD for the first and last time a few hours before. These few extracts say it all:

> I never fully realized the rhythm of the thing — oh, I did intellectually, the cycle of birth, growth, decay, death. Growth always seemed to be at the peak. I don't want to make a virtue of death but right now they all are at the same level. Decay and death, are no less than birth and growth. Can this be the final rationalization? Hardly. At this moment values don't matter. Life and death matter — they are of me.

Or again —

> When I die, I won't be remembered long — there aren't many friends and hardly any relatives left. Nothing much accomplished — no children — nothing. But that's all right, too.[26]

The psychiatrist never did anything with the tapes of that afternoon. He never wrote the book or article. He felt that the whole LSD issue had become absurd, over-popularized and potentially dangerous to a professional reputation. In view of Timothy Leary's psychedelic circus, the strict federal controls and the recent finding of chromosome damage, he is certainly justified in his position. For those very reasons I had never recommended, as a teacher or as a friend, the taking of LSD. But I do think it is time a few "thin skulls" began to speak up. The thick skulls are right about the dangers of the cube bought in Greenwich Village, the un-monitored trip, and repeated usage. They also, instinctively and brutally, will do all they can to preserve our present society of fear and greed. To them visions are far more dangerous than Vietnam. After my own overwhelming experience three years ago, in view of our continuing society of cut-throat, competitive compatibility, and putting my own reputation now on the line, I feel that every teacher, every artist, every psychologist, every clergyman and every superior student should be permitted to have the experience *once*.

---

[26] Sidney Cohen, "L.S.D. and the Anguish of Dying," *Harper's Magazine*, September, 1965, 34.

I'm aware how preposterous such a suggestion seems. As a "rather cautious academic type," I shock myself when I follow my thinking to its logical conclusion. I am proposing an "acid elite." Those who seem promising but can't measure up to the confrontation of self with the "other" are still caught in the old society of fear and greed. They should not hold positions of responsibility until they indicate that their educations as human beings have really taken, that they are themselves creative and/or are able to appreciate creation.

Can it be that after only one trip I have suffered irreversible brain damage myself? The damage, I think, was done long before, in college, in my religious training. I was taught to seek out moments of spiritual-physical enlightenment by people who had never experienced them. If anything, my one trip righted the balance of expectation and disappointment. Even so thick-skulled — or let's say, level-headed — an observer as Diana Trilling, in the midst of a negative *Encounter* criticism of Timothy Leary's Celebrations in the Village, admitted that "L.S.D. would seem to have a gentling effect on the personality. I have observed this curious transformation in all the young people I know who have taken the drug; even after only one or two trips they attain a sort of suprahumanity, as if they had been purged of mortal error; and as far as I can make out, this change persists."[27]

The insight obtained seems too great to be missed; it is tantamount to a reorganization of perception that permits the properly prepared individual to experience a creative, aesthetic and religious moment that can never be forgotten. I have only the vaguest suggestions as to how the trip would be arranged. Once it was a custom after graduation from college to go on a grand tour of Europe. Perhaps we could establish the custom of a post-graduation grand trip of the mind. I assume the government could be persuaded once again to permit Sandoz Pharmaceuticals to produce uncontaminated LSD, that boards of psychiatrists, artists and teachers who already have had the experience, would judge

[27] Diana Trilling, "Celebrating with Dr. Leary," *Encounter*, June, 1967.

which graduating students were mature enough for the trip, and that the surroundings and safeguards in taking the trip would be like those I was fortunate enough to have. It would be the final examination before graduation, the acid test. As I have noted already, the word "education" comes from the Latin "ex" and "ducere"; i.e., to lead out. In its powers of releasing the potentialities for appreciation in the normal human being LSD should be seen as no more a manipulation of the psyche than any other educational tool.

CHAPTER V

God Is Functioning:
Buber, Bonhoeffer, and Dewart

FRIDAY'S CHILD

(In memory of Dietrich Bonhoeffer, martyred at
Flossenberg, April 9, 1945)

He told us we were free to choose
But, children as we were, we thought —
"Paternal Love will only use
    Force in the last resort

On those too bumptious to repent" —
Accustomed to religious dread,
It never crossed our minds He meant
    Exactly what He said.

Perhaps He frowns, perhaps He grieves,
But it seems idle to discuss
If angel or compassion leaves
    The bigger bangs to us.

What reverence is rightly paid
To a Divinity so odd
He lets the Adam whom He made
    Perform the Acts of God?

It might be jolly if we felt
Awe at this Universal Man;
(When kings were local, people knelt)
    Some try to, but who can?

The self-observed observing Mind
We meet when we observe at all
Is not alarming or unkind
    But utterly banal.

Though instruments at Its command
Make wish and counterwish come true,
It clearly cannot understand
    What It can clearly do.

Since the analogies are rot
Our senses based belief upon,
We have no means of learning what
    Is really going on,

And must put up with having learned
All proofs or disproofs that we tender
Of His existence are returned
     Unopened to the sender.

Now, did He really break the seal
And rise again? We dare not say;
But conscious unbelievers feel
     Quite sure of Judgment Day.

Meanwhile, a silence on the cross,
As dead as we shall ever be,
Speaks of some total gain or loss,
     And you and I are free

To guess from the insulted face
Just what Appearances He saves
     By suffering in a public place
A death reserved for slaves.
               W. H. Auden (*Homage to Clio*)*

In this, my final chapter, I draw together three thinkers each
of whom has a theological message of convergence, and all
of whom demonstrate a wide spectrum of convergence. I
focus first upon Martin Buber, a Jew whose culture is altogether Germanic but whose thought is anchored profoundly
in his biblical and Hebraic inheritance. His thought, it seems
to me, is summed up in the title of his most moving book,
I and Thou. Though this work was first published in 1927,
it continues to be discussed. Indeed it has only been since the
Second World War that its wider implications have been
explored. Next, I deal with the Lutheran minister, Dietrich
Bonhoeffer, who in 1945 was hanged by the Gestapo for
having been an active member in a band of conspirators that
plotted the assassination of Hitler. His notes and letters,
written while he was languishing in a Nazi cell, were collected
posthumously under the title *Letters and Papers from Prison*.
The book, though fragmentary, has had a direct influence
upon the "Death of God" theologians. Finally I turn to
Leslie Dewart's *The Future of Belief*. Dewart is probably
one of the most radical of modern Catholic theologians. He
does not believe that the Hellenic notions of being or person

---

* New York: Random House, 1960.

can be meaningfully predicated of God, preferring to conceive of God as the intangible reality underlying and undergirding the universe and heaven-consciousness.

All three of these theologians stress our responsibility for reconstructing this earth, and their emphasis on human responsibility indicates perhaps a tendency toward Pelagianism, although it might be better to describe this as a Promethean tendency. Though each of them would agree "that ordinary human experience is insufficient unless it extends itself into a new extraordinary dimension" (Dewart), each also is a secular thinker working out his salvation in the temporal order. The aspects of their work which *incline toward* Manichaeanism—far more elusive, perhaps even illusive— will be pointed out in the course of the chapter. Each of these men is in love with the works of this world, because they see the world transformed through the dissolving of arbitrary lines of demarcation between the so-called sacred and profane. My emphasis will be on the convergence taking place. Thus, throughout this chapter, I will refer to previous chapters to underscore the wide secular implications of their thinking.

Buber's thinking on human as well as divine-human relationships is compressed in his two sets of formulae: I-It and I-Thou. The point of these distinctions may seem obvious, but this ease of understanding is deceptive. When I am confronted with a person I react differently than I do when I am concerned with things; I cannot know, nor desire, nor love an "it" in the same way as I do a "thou." In the world of "I-It," the "I" passes among things, deals with the surface, at most has an experience, never a relationship. The "It" does nothing to the experience itself; it is solely an "I" experience of "it," and the world has no part in it, save that it allows itself to be experienced. When we say "It" we mean also other persons insofar as we treat them as things. The scientist, the doctor, the philosopher, the economist, the employer, all usually do this. In our ordinary life our acquaintances are

experienced not as persons but as things. Whenever, in fact, we use the third person we are doing this. Of course, Buber acknowledges that none of us can live on an "I-Thou" level at all times, but it is important to have the insight.

I-Thou represents the profoundest convergence. When the Victorian poet-priest, Gerard Manley Hopkins, writes of inscape and instress, he touches upon this very relationship. One can look at a tree and conjecture how much money it would bring on the lumber market, or how many chairs could be made from it. But when Hopkins sees trees being cut down in "Binsey Poplars" he can weep, for he has felt the instress of their relationship with him, has known the inscape of their presence on the landscape. Here again is the "prehensive unity," the event connected to everything else that seems to have influenced Buckminster Fuller. And on the human relationship level, "I-Thou" is the jeweled pivot upon which swings all real meaning. In such a relationship the human being is not "a nature to be experienced and described but . . . whole in himself, he is Thou and fills the heaven. . . . All else lives in his light." Buber says that the word "experience" is wrong when used of a Thou; there is a relation, but it is one of meeting — a meeting of fulfillment for both. "The primary word I-Thou can be spoken only with the whole being. Concentration and fusion into the whole being can never take place through my agency, nor can it ever take place without me. I become through my relation to the Thou; as I become I, I say Thou. All real living is meeting."[1] Thus you can never be yourself in a world of things. The "I-Thou" convergence is necessary to realize yourself. Only in crying "Thou" can you become I. Otherwise you are an It. Buber expresses this splendidly in a passage which demonstrates how far his own "I-Thou" insight has taken him: "Love is responsibility of an I for a Thou. In this lies the likeness . . . of all who love, from the smallest to the greatest and from the blessedly protected man, whose

[1] Martin Buber, *I and Thou* (New York: Charles Scribner's Sons, 1958), pp. 3, 11.

life is rounded in that of a loved being, to him who is all his life nailed to a cross and who ventures to bring himself to the dreadful point — to love *all men*."[2]

Buber describes how in infancy the child first contacts the world and has to find for himself the meaning of that world. At this point in one's life the world is a thing to be grappled with rather than related to. "The development of the soul in the child is inextricably bound up with that of the longing for the Thou, with the satisfaction and the disappointment of this longing, with the games of his experiments and the tragic seriousness of his perplexity."[3] When the child finally manages to meet the Thou of the world, when he manages "the separation of the body from the world round about it," he himself becomes an "I." During this time, he experiences the "integration of being" which Fuller and Brown so admire in the four-year-old child. He is a part of the universe, knowing himself to be an entity, but accepting all things and beings as of equal value and interest. However the will becomes stronger, the ego asserts itself, and soon the links of the I-Thou relationship are broken to be replaced by the limited I-It experience. Buber is describing the archetypal story of the loss of Paradise, in which man gains rational control only to discover that he is now able to experience anxiety in his anticipation of tomorrow and death. And in describing the "I-Thou" relationship he is suggesting how we can regain that Paradise if only for brief moments. I have no intention of belittling Buber's insight when I suggest that Alan Watts, in describing his perspectives on the world seen with the help of eastern disciplines and/or hallucinatory drugs, seems to be recounting the same kind of event.

Much that I have written about Teilhard applies to Buber's thoughts on "I-Thou." Of course, Buber is dealing with one person meeting another person rather than the ultimate universal convergence, but even the noosphere is made up of individual minds and the "continuous man" has individual

---

[2] *Ibid.*, p. 273.
[3] *Ibid.*, p. 27.

cells. Both, however, are aware that "hell" is the ego separated from creation, from the beings and things of the universe. For both we free ourselves from hell by being and seeing others not as individuals but as persons. Buber writes, for
example, that it is possible for a business leader to fill his
business with dialogue by meeting the men with whom he
works as persons. "Even when he cannot meet them directly,
he can be inwardly aware, with a latent and disciplined
fantasy, of the multitudes of these persons, so that when one
of them does step before him as an individual, he can meet
him not as a number with a human mask but as a person."[4]
And Teilhard, when explaining that the ultimate convergence
is a loss of individuality but not of personality, makes a distinction that Buber would readily accept. In *The Phenomenon of Man* Teilhard writes:

> Egoism . . . feels right. Its only mistake, but a fatal one, is
> *to confuse individuality with personality.* In trying to separate
> itself as much as possible from others, the element individualises
> itself. . . . In fact it diminishes itself and loses itself. To be
> fully ourselves it is in the opposite direction, in the direction
> of convergence with all the rest, that we must advance — towards
> the other. The goal of ourselves, the acme of our originality,
> is not our individuality but our person; and according to the
> evolutionary structure of the world, we can only find our person
> by uniting together. There is no mind without synthesis.[5]

Teilhard emphasizes the I-Thou relationship when he adds:
"For the human particles to become really personalized under the creative influence of union, they must not . . . join
up together anyhow. Since it is a question of achieving a
synthesis of centres, it is centre to centre that they must contact and not otherwise."[6]

Buber shared with Teilhard a love of nature that seems at
times almost pantheistic. He writes in an article, "Ueber
Jakob Böhme" (1901), that "God is not divided but everywhere whole, and where he reveals himself, there he is wholly

---

[4] Buber, *Between Man and Man* (London: Kegan Paul, 1947), p. 20.
[5] Pierre Teilhard de Chardin, *The Phenomenon of Man* (New York:
Harper & Row, 1959), p. 263.
[6] *Ibid.*

present." It is an experience of world-feeling which becomes woven in our own experience. Maurice Friedman, probably the soundest of Buber scholars, describes Buber's mysticism as a sense of identity with nature in which we feel "the desire to put our arm around a young tree and feel the same surge of life as in ourselves or to read our own most special mystery in the eyes of a dumb animal. We experience the ripening and fading of far-distant stars as something which happens to us, and there are moments in which our organism is a wholly other piece of nature."[7] Buber can claim in the same article that "Man with man — the unity of I and Thou — is God." And he can speak of a "Face" that is sometimes seen, briefly, when one looks deep into the eyes of a finite Thou.

But there is in Buber's thinking a fear of the progressive augmentation of the world of "It" which is almost Manichaean in its implications. He sees the world of spirit, of I-Thou, being replaced by the world of matter, of institutions. The world of I-It may provide order and continuity and therefore be of value in man's day-to-day existence, but if this world of appearance, of gross matter replaces the spiritual relationships between men, then the significance has gone out of life. As with the Romantic poets and with Hopkins, Buber fears that man may forget how to feel:

> Institutions are "outside," where all sorts of aims are pursued, where a man works, negotiates, bears influence, undertakes, organizes, conducts business, officiates, preaches. . . . Feelings are "within," where life is lived and man recovers from institutions. Here the spectrum of the emotions dances before the interested glance.[8]

Out of this institutional world comes the self-willed man who recognizes no connection other than force and cash. He is self-willed, yet the irony is that he is defined and limited by things. His sphere of influence is circumscribed by his material ego and thus he has no destiny for he has no real end

[7] Maurice Friedman, *Martin Buber: The Life of Dialogue* (New York: Harper & Row, 1960), p. 28.

[8] Buber, *I and Thou*, p. 43.

other than immediate gratification. In the final analysis, Buber's I and Thou can be equated with Teilhard's radial energy; I and It can be related to the priest-philosopher's tangential energy. I-It and tangential energy chronicle the disintegration of culture through inertia, while I-Thou and radial energy concentrate and refocus culture through love.

It is the "world of it" that introduces evil into the world, but the confrontation with evil can reveal the real will of man, not self-will, but conscious cooperation with the evolving world. On the issues of evil and man's will Buber and Teilhard seem to be in agreement. In a lecture on the Tao, Buber sees the story of Adam's fall as a parable of man's need for evil:

> The dynamic of man, that which man as man has to fulfill, is unthinkable without evil. Man first became man through being driven out of Paradise. Good and evil form together the body of the world. If man had simply to live in the good, then there would be no work of man. That work is: to make the broken world whole. Paradise is at the lower end of separateness, but in order that its upper part, the kingdom, the great peace and unification, come, evil is necessary. . . . Evil is the hardness which divides being from being, being from God. The act of decision, of breakthrough . . . that is the act through which man time and again participates in the redemption of the world.[9]

This interpretation parallels Teilhard's views of energy working its way through and transforming the barrier of matter. Though Teilhard has little to say about evil, the concluding section of The Phenomenon of Man seems to present evil — even the evil flowing out of man's self-will — as potential good. He writes that "Suffering and failure, tears and blood: so many by-products (often precious, moreover, and re-utilisable) begotten by the noosphere on its way. . . . In one manner or the other it still remains true that, even in the view of the mere biologist, the human epic resembles nothing so much as a way of the Cross."[10]

For both thinkers man is able to will his own future. Here

---

[9] Buber, "The Teaching of the Tao," Pointing the Way (New York: Harper & Row, 1957), p. 32.

[10] Teilhard de Chardin, op. cit., p. 311.

we may detect a tendency toward Pelagianism, but of course, with qualification, since both of them saw the millennium or the Noosphere as the ultimate, though as yet, undefined goal of man as well as the *intention of God*. Still, this shared emphasis upon the will of man reveals a fundamental way in which Buber is related not only to Teilhard but to the other two Christian theologians dealt with in this chapter. Religion has always been the record of man's attempt to return to paradise. In the past, Christianity promised this paradise, this realization of peace, security, tranquility, prosperity, in the future, beyond this life. The present climate of opinion gravitates round a paradise to be realized here and now. Judaism, on the other hand, has always expected the millennium on this earth, a millennium that man must bring about through his own efforts with the blessing of God. Fuller's integrated man and integrated structures, Bazelon's world of moneyless abundance, Brown's garden of uninhibited pleasure, all are various manifestations of what Cox called "the Secular City" — and all of them are suggesting a utopia brought about through man's own efforts.

Buber's secular vision seems sharper and more immediately practical than Teilhard's. Coming as he does from the Hasidic tradition, he is profoundly directed toward an affirmation of man's life on earth. For him there is no secular life and holy life; all life is holy. As a Hasidic Jew he reacted against the letter of the law established by orthodox Judaism and put his faith in a fellowship of men making God real in their midst. He felt that a social restructuring of society was necessary because capitalism with its cash nexus rationale of competition eventually destroyed any inclination toward organic community. Nor does he have any faith in Marxism since its goals of freedom and multiplicity can never be allowed because of the pressure of centralization. Capitalism, Marxism, and Fascism all eventually subordinate the individual to the institution and thus make it impossible to build a society based on I-Thou relationships. Buber offers Utopian Socialism as the best answer in a world which must have a healthy alternation between the order and system of "I-It" and the relationship of "I-Thou." "True socialism," he writes in *Paths in Utopia*, "is real community between men, direct life-relationship between I and Thou, just society and fellowship."[11]

Such a state cannot take place through the blind working of economic forces or even through Bazelon's total production. There has to be human will behind it; there has to be a setting up of a goal and the willingness to will and work that goal into a reality. As Maurice Friedman puts it in *Martin Buber: The Life of Dialogue*, "This goal is based on the longing for rightness — the vision of perfection that in religious expectation takes the form of Messianism — perfection in time — and in social expectation the form of Utopia — perfection in space."[12] Such a society grows out of the needs, the traditions, the shared memories, the tribal closeness of the people. It grows out of the shared experiences of relationships which sometimes at least can be I-Thou encounters. Buber insists that it is a tragic mistake to start the organization of society from general principles and then apply them to individuals. Such a society is one of closed morality imposing a world of It upon its members. He proposes the creation of communities through individual relatedness, and these communes would themselves converge in a large community with, however, each smaller community preserving its autonomy. Essentially, he is taking the individual-person distinction worked out on the man to man level and applying it to the social level. Such a society is a dynamic ever-changing one whose fundamentals are "a restricting of society as a League of Leagues," "a reduction of the State to its proper function, which is to maintain unity," and the continuous establishing of "the right proportion . . . between group-freedom and collective order."

Buber holds that the full cooperative community is the only answer. This would be a community which combines industry and agriculture, production and consumption around

---

[11] Buber, *Paths to Utopia* (Boston: Beacon Press, 1958), p. 139.
[12] Friedman, *op. cit.*, p. 211.

community-held land. The plan reminds me of the Haight-Asbury diggers' projected farm communities, and it certainly suggests how society might work if it were freed from what David Bazelon calls "The Paper Economy." Apparently Buber felt that the most promising experiment in the village cooperative community was to be found in the Jewish communes in Palestine. The members of these groups, according to Buber, display an "amazingly positive relationship — amounting to a regular faith — to the inmost being of their commune."[13] This seems to be Buber's real faith, a faith in the person and the society developing out of the relationship of persons who refuse the anthill of conformity or the hell of total individualism. To Buber the kabutz was a living community in which each member had to be willing to open his heart to the feelings and thoughts of the others. Without that close relationship the whole experiment could be a hopeless, frightening experiment in indoctrination, not at all unlike B. F. Skinner's misguided, conditioned world in *Walden II*, where children separated from their families were brainwashed into accepting what was good for the community. As long as the dialogue in the community continued Buber had no fear. "The coming state of humanity in the great crisis," said Buber in 1952, "depends very much on whether another type of socialism can be set up against Moscow and I venture even today to call it Jerusalem."[14]

Buber's influence upon modern thinkers is appreciable enough that Harvey Cox found it necessary to deal directly with the I-Thou relationship and in part transform it into a formula that could work in the Secular City. Cox maintains that theologians and social philosophers often fortify their reservations about modern modes of life with wistful references to Buber's I-Thou relationship. Cox holds that because of the flexibility, mobility, and ease of communication in modern urban cities we do not build up relationships on the arbitrary basis of propinquity. He hastens to add:

[13] Buber, *Paths to Utopia*, p. 42.
[14] From an address on Israel given by Professor Buber at the Jewish Theological Seminary of America, New York, April 1, 1952.

This does not mean the apartment dweller cannot love his nextdoor neighbor. He can and often does so, certainly no less frequently than the small-town resident. But he does so by being a dependable fellow tenant, by bearing his share of the common responsibility they both have in that segment of their lives shaped by residence. This does not require their becoming cronies.[15]

Cox rejoices in the new community, not based on geographic lines but on interest. He may not yet foresee McLuhan's "global tribe," but he does welcome the megapolis where a man may share space with five million individuals and single out from that mass of people a community of twenty-five persons with whom he relates closely, perhaps even in an I-Thou camaraderie. Cox observes that to treat every person with whom you come in contact as a Thou would be exhausting. He offers an alternative: "Why could we not evolve a theology of the I-You relationship? Such a relationship would cover the very human but nonpersonal contacts we all make in any given day in a large city."[16] The nonmetaphysical Cox has no more a mystique of the past, of ritual and of place, than he has a vision of a paradise in the sky. His paradise is to be realized here and now and it is in our grasp. "The development of an I-You theology," he believes, "would greatly clarify the human possibilities of urban life, and would help stall attempts to lure urban people back into preurban conviviality under the color of saving their souls."[17]

Cox presents the picture of a relatively young and affluent theological playboy savoring rather than saving the city. However, I fear he dismisses the family neighborhood units too quickly. Buber is wise in talking about the whole man, human both in body and mind, human whether young and mobile or old and poor. His vision of the integrated community echoes Wordsworth's ideas on the value of a family group living together, teaching each other by example how to live and how to die. The search for roots, for ground to stand on,

---

[15] Harvey Cox, *The Secular City* (New York: Macmillan, 1965), p. 45.
[16] *Ibid.*, pp. 48–49.
[17] *Ibid.*

seems to have escaped Cox entirely. However, even if one takes the world on Cox's terms, the convergence is there. The tribe may not have roots but it has antennae, and according to McLuhan is participating in instantaneous and simultaneous communication. Still it is significant that before becoming a spokesman for pop-art and mobility, McLuhan was a scholar who wrote well about the inscape and instress of Gerard Manley Hopkins' poetry. Recall that a few pages back I equated Hopkins' inscape/instress with Buber's I-Thou formula. I suspect that McLuhan and Cox are both aware that much of the electronic world of communication may touch all surfaces simultaneously, but that it only touches the surfaces. The real need is for the kind of convergent relationships Buber described. Cox's I-You distinction is misleading, for Buber never taught that it was possible to have an I-Thou relationship with everybody. Rather he felt that there was an eternal human need, "the need of man to feel his own house as a room in some greater, all-embracing structure in which he is at home, to feel that the other inhabitants of it with whom he lives and works are all acknowledging and confirming his individual existence."[18] The fulfillment of this need led to a man who was more likely to give and have the I-Thou relationship. And though he might have the experience only occasionally his whole attitude toward his fellow human beings would be transformed.

Buber was opposed to the closed morality resulting from a dogmatic approach to God. As futile as the attempt to set up a rigid pattern for the I-Thou relationship is the attempt to force an encounter with God. Buber never assumed a "God is Dead" position, but he did analyze the problems that led up to this position and he indicated that the solution rested in a true understanding of his relational formulae. Buber sees the will of modern man caught in a self-enclosed world of "It" which prevents him from experiencing anyone but himself. His analysis is almost a theological gloss of Conrad's *Heart of Darkness*:

---

[18] Buber, *Paths to Utopia*, p. 139.

> In our age the I-It relation, gigantically swollen, has usurped
> . . . the mastery and the rule. The I of this relation . . .
> unable to meet a being essentially, is the lord of the hour.
> This selfhood that has become omnipotent, with all the It
> around it, can naturally acknowledge neither God nor any
> genuine absolute which manifests itself to man as of nonhuman
> origin.[19]

One recalls how Kurtz's reiterated "I," "I," became a final
"The horror, the horror."

It is in the relationship of "I" to God's Thou that one
frees oneself from this horror. Again, all that has been said
about the relation of man to man applies here as well, only
on a more intense level. For Buber "the description of God
as a Person is indispensable." God is the Person "who — whatever else he may be — enters into a direct relation with us
men in creative, revealing and redeeming acts and thus makes
it possible for us to enter into a direct relation with him.
This ground and meaning of our existence constitutes a
mutuality, arising again and again, such as can subsist only
between persons." In this extension of the I-Thou relation,
Buber is able to envisage man discovering the possibilities of
his own person through God. Of course, God, too, is an "I" in
this relation and consequently one can logically see God as
realizing His possibilities through man. This divine-human
mutuality is paralleled in Teilhard's thesis that man's evolution permits God to become manifest. Because of the insights
derived from this relationship, Buber sees God both as a
Being outside man and thus transcendent and within man
and thus immanent. When Buber tells us that God is limited
"by the plurality of other independent entities," he would
seem to be going even further than Teilhard; he would seem
to be claiming that God is the sum total of all human
energy manifested in spirit, mind and matter. Thus "realization," what Christians call "salvation," is to be found in
recognizing our godhead in others, in developing living, working, playing relationships with them.

---

[19] Buber, "God and the Spirit of Man," *Eclipse of God* (New York:
Harper & Row, 1952), p. 165.

By a logical Christian extension of Buber's thinking, one could postulate that in the I-Thou relation of God and man, the person of Jesus Christ would be the initial and ultimate path of realization. Such a view informs Teilhard's thinking when he writes that "Christ invests himself organically with the very majesty of his creation. . . . To be able to say literally to God that one loves him, not only with all one's body, all one's heart and all one's soul, but with every fibre of the unifying universe — that is a prayer that can only be made in space-time."[20] For Teilhard it is the fact that Christ incorporated Himself in matter that permits us to evolve as we come in contact with His creation. "I have tried to show," Teilhard writes, "that we can hope for no progress on earth without the primacy and triumph of the personal."[21] Such a statement seems almost pure Buber. Indeed I doubt that that magnanimous Jewish thinker would have been unduly irritated with such an extension. He himself wrote in *Two Types of Faith*:

> From my youth onwards I have found in Jesus my great brother. That Christianity has regarded and does regard him as God and Saviour has always appeared to me a fact of the highest importance which, for his sake and my own, I must endeavour to understand. . . . My own fraternally open relationship to him has grown ever stronger and clearer, and today I see him more strongly and clearly than ever before. I am more than ever certain that a great place belongs to him in Israel's history of faith and that this place cannot be described by any of the usual categories.[22]

It is this notion of the immanence of God seen at least obliquely in Buber that informs the secularity of Cox as well as the more theologically guarded statements of Bonhoeffer and Dewart. For them as for many modern theologians, God is our neighbor who needs our help, and it is we who must continue to evolve through a constant relationship with creation.

---

[20] Teilhard de Chardin, *op. cit.*, p. 297.
[21] *Ibid.*
[22] Buber, *Two Types of Faith* (New York: Macmillan Company, 1952), p. 12.

The modified immanentism of Buber and Teilhard is not innately unorthodox. There are passages in Saint Paul and Saint John that corroborate this view of man, passages to which Teilhard refers in his exposition of the evolution of man-God. It is a matter of emphasis. Both the Jewish thinker and the Jesuit scientist are cautious and ultimately orthodox in their balancing of immanentism with an ever-present awareness of a transcendent being. Bonhoeffer and Dewart, on the other hand, are less cautious. They both seem to believe that for all practical purposes — and all their purposes are practical — the transcendental God is dead. Buber says "God is in eclipse"; they see Him buried, buried inside of the creatures He has made, but always on the verge of resurrection through man's properly directed will.

Martin E. Marty has written in *The Place of Bonhoeffer*: "Younger European and American Christian thinkers often seem to be divided into two camps: those who acknowledge their debt to Bonhoeffer and those who are indebted but who obscure the traces to their source."[23] This considerable influence rests largely on his posthumously published notes and letters. One of the central passages deals with the need for a rejection of a religious interpretation of Christianity:

> In my view [a religious interpretation] means to speak on the one hand metaphysically and on the other hand individualistically. Neither of these is relevant to the Bible message or to the man of today. Is it not true to say that individualistic concern for personal salvation has almost completely left us all? Are we not really under the impression that there are more important things than bothering about such a matter? (Perhaps not more important than the matter itself, but more than bothering about it.) I know it sounds pretty monstrous to say that. But is it not, at bottom, even biblical? Is there any concern in the Old Testament about saving one's soul at all? Is not righteousness and the Kingdom of God on earth the focus of everything, and is not Romans 3:14 ff., too, the culmination of the view that in God alone is righteousness, and not in an individualistic doctrine of salvation? It is not

23 Martin E. Marty, *The Place of Bonhoeffer* (New York: Association Press, 1962), p. 10.

with the next world that we are concerned, but with this world. . . .[24]

As in Buber, there is an emphasis upon work and relationship in this world rather than on an "individualistic doctrine of salvation." In that sense, he is a secular theologian, one whom Cox quotes extensively in *The Secular City.*

He was a secularist in his willingness to be involved in politics. He shared with the Hasidic Jews an unwillingness to make a distinction between the secular and the sacred, feeling that the line of demarcation had been drawn in the Renaissance and drawn because of gross misconceptions. He held that man must plunge himself into the destructive element, "into the life of a godless world." "He must live a worldly life and so participate in the suffering of God. . . . To be a Christian does not mean to be religious in a particular way, to cultivate some particular form of asceticism . . . but to be a man. It is not some religious act which makes a Christian what he is, but participation in the suffering of God in the life of the world."[25]

His actions during the Nazi tyranny make it clear how fully he was willing to participate in those sufferings. Although he was in America in 1939, he decided to return to Germany because, as he wrote to American friends, "I will have no right to participate in the reconstruction of Christian life in Germany after the war if I do not share the trials of this time with my people. . . . Christians in Germany will face the terrible alternative of either willing the defeat of their nation in order that Christian civilization may survive or willing the victory of their nation and thereby destroying our civilization. I know which of those alternatives I must choose, but I cannot make that choice in security."[26]

From the very first, he was aware of the moral and physical horror Hitler represented. Hitler became chancellor on Jan-

---

[24] Dietrich Bonhoeffer, *Letters and Papers from Prison* (New York: The Macmillan Company, 1953), pp. 167–168.

[25] *Ibid.,* pp. 222–223.

[26] Bonhoeffer, *The Way to Freedom* (New York: Harper & Row, 1966), p. 246.

uary 30, 1933. On February 1, Bonhoeffer was cut off the radio in the midst of a broadcast in which he was criticizing the "leadership principle." When the opportunity came to join a select group of conspirators in an attempt to assassinate Hitler, Bonhoeffer was secular enough to know that religious scruples did not give him the right *not* to kill.

As with Sartre and Camus, he found that each one of us is forced to work out his own code of ethics in a world in which religion-established Christianity has become outmoded, in which, as Auden puts it, the Divinity "lets the Adam whom He made/ Perform the Acts of God." In his earlier works he was relatively orthodox, but during 1943–1944 — those two years in a Nazi jail, he arrived at a position that might be called Christian existentialism. Even as the existentialist holds that we must establish "a clean well-lighted place" in the midst of darkness and meaninglessness, that we must engage ourselves in practical activity that seems meaningful, so Bonhoeffer held that we cannot encounter the reality of God except by commitment to concrete, worldly matters. This is the religion of heroism that Bazelon and Cox write of. It is a religion of responsibility. Christians must "dare to look into the future." The "final responsible question," wrote Bonhoeffer, is "how a coming generation shall continue to live."

Strictly speaking, I shouldn't use such phrases as "religion of responsibility," "religion of heroism," when discussing Bonhoeffer, for his quintessential message is that we must live as "religionless Christians." To him religion meant a special feeling, a special badge that — using Buber's terms — could make the person into an individual. Bonhoeffer distrusted such unthinking religious commitment; in the forefront of ecumenism in his day, he felt that Christianity was not rubrics but relatedness, not conversion but convergence. Restricted and labeled religion was an excuse not to relate. It was an excuse to stop living existentially and to rest your responsibility on the narrow shoulders of recognized authority. Only by divorcing ourselves from dogmatic, ritualistic religion can we begin to find answers to the real questions:

1. "What is the significance of a Church in a religionless world?"
2. "In what way are we in a religionless and secular sense Christian?"
3. "How do we speak . . . in secular fashion of God?"[27]

Perhaps the three questions can be resolved to one of Buber's. Late in his life the rabbi is reported to have said: "I often hear men say they would gladly throw away the world. Is the world yours to throw away?"

Bonhoeffer's answer to the first question is direct enough:

> The Church is her true self only when she exists for humanity. As a fresh start she should give away all her endowments to the poor and needy. The clergy should live solely on the free-will offerings of their congregations, or possibly engage in some secular calling. She must take her part in the social life of the world, not lording it over men, but helping and serving them. She must tell men, whatever their calling, what it means to live in Christ, to exist for others.[28]

The Church, then, is a spirit rather than an institution. "Upon this rock" — Peter, the human being — "shall I build my Church." It should be a catalyst or better yet, to use Coleridge's term, an esemplastic factor; i.e., a factor that forms being and enters into that being itself. The being formed is one of convergence, one that recognizes the divine energy in its laity as well as in its sacramental ministers, one capable of divesting itself of worldly ostentation, while welcoming the joys and creaturely comforts this world can provide for all. Its message *is* its mission. It speaks through the spirit rather than through the letter, through action rather than catechisms. "By its fruits — not its prohibitions and renunciations — shall you know it."

This nonmaterial Church working in a material world, rather than the customary inversion, leads to the second question posed by Bonhoeffer. His answer is in part influenced by Buber. Bonhoeffer observes that "God encounters us not only as a Thou, but also disguised as an It; so in the last

---

[27] Bonhoeffer, *Letters and Papers* . . . , p. 164.
[28] *Ibid.*, p. 239.

resort my question is how we are to find the Thou in this It
(i.e., fate). In other words, how does fate become providence?"[29] We redeem our time from insignificance by not trying to redeem it at all. Instead of waging a battle for religion
against the world — which is what religion has been doing
since the Renaissance — we must wage our battle for a better
world against the forces of secular evil. We must be capable
of a generous anger which will reverse Yeats' grim observation
that "the best lack all conviction, while the worst are full
of a passionate intensity." Bonhoeffer's scruples did not prevent his attempt on Hitler's life. He was in the world
and of the world and he knew action had to be taken
to transform fate into providence. Fate and Providence? Isn't
this simply a way of saying the secular world is transformed
into the sacred through man's committed involvement? All
religious encouragements to perceive human events *sub specie
aeternitatis*, to rest your burdens in the Lord, he saw as fatal
short-circuitings of human energy. Creation should be en-
countered in all its "itness." The arrival at insight, at enlightenment when the disguise falls and the Thou is seen, requires
an unconditional entrance into the finite and the limited.
Now, of course, such a policy is an activist one, yet oddly
enough it is also related to the passive eastern approaches to
enlightenment. In both, the major block to attaining insight
or enlightenment is to have from the very start a consciousness of the end, to assume that there is something more important than the experience you are having at this moment.
Again in Auden's words we must be prepared to encounter a
world that "Is not alarming or unkind/ But utterly banal."
The world of It becomes Thou only by accepting the It.
Auden puts it well in his Christmas Oratorio, *For The Time
Being*. He writes of those who have had the moment of
enlightenment when

> Everything became a You and nothing was an It. . . .
> We look round for something, no matter what, to inhibit
> Our self-reflection. . . . In the meantime

---

[29] *Ibid.*, p. 138.

> There are bills to be paid, machines to keep in repair
> Irregular verbs to learn, the Time Being to redeem
> From insignificance.[30]

Bonhoeffer believed in a relaxing of the will on the metaphysical level so that the will might work more fully on the physical:

> It is only by living completely in this world that one learns to believe. One must abandon every attempt to make something of oneself, whether it be a saint, a converted sinner, a churchman, a righteous man, or an unrighteous one. . . . This is what I mean by worldliness — taking life in one's stride, with all its duties and problems, its successes and failures, its experiences and helplessness.[31]

This passage, together with his views on the need to confront the finite rather than presuming to engage the supernatural, follow logically from his position in *The Cost of Discipleship* (1937) that "Cheap grace is the deadly enemy of our Church. We are fighting today for costly grace."[32] "Cheap grace" was the result of accepting an institution's assurances that merit could be obtained by ceremony. Costly grace was the product of a willingness to die if needs be for a secular cause one knew to be just and good.

Even in the confined life of a Nazi cell, Bonhoeffer demonstrated a life lived in terms of costly grace. In the midst of a Kafka-like nightmare of waiting month after month for a trial that never took place, Bonhoeffer not only wrote his letters and notes which further clarified his phrase "costly grace," but he also tested that belief. In the midst of bombing raids, he remained calm and useful, helping to minister to the sick and injured, offering not by words but by deeds grounds for hope. Indeed his only serious complaint about his fellow prisoners is that a few among them were cowardly in the face of physical danger and revealed "a kind of weakness Christianity will not stand for." But the real grace, the

---

[30] W. H. Auden, *For the Time Being* (New York: Random House, Inc., 1944), p. 131.

[31] Bonhoeffer, *Letters and Papers* . . . , p. 226.

[32] Bonhoeffer, *The Cost of Discipleship* (New York: The Macmillan Company, 1964), p. 47.

kind that distinguishes Bonhoeffer as a secular Christian, is revealed in his acceptance of the atheists and agnotics around him. He reports that he often shrank from speaking God's name before the "religious" but "with people who have no religion I am able on occasion to speak of God quite openly and, as it were, naturally."[33]

What does a Lutheran minister who is aspiring to become a religionless Christian in a non-institutional Church have to say about God to atheists? This is Bonhoeffer's third question. There is one kind of God Bonhoeffer is not interested in, the kind of God that is invoked "when human perception is . . . at an end, or human resources fail: it is really always the *Deus ex machina* they call to their aid, either for the so-called solving of insoluble problems or as support in human failure."[34] Only by abandoning this notion of God can men come to depend on each other, can they come to find the God within them. In writing of the separation of friends Bonhoeffer touches on this need for the absence of God. He holds that the very gap left unfilled preserves and confirms the bonds of friendship. "It is nonsense to say that God fills the gap: he does not fill it, but keeps it empty so that our communion with another may be kept alive even at the cost of pain."[35] This absence of a deistic God forces man to find his real self in the other. Bonhoeffer's spatial separation may, I think, be legitimately extended to the psychological separation we experience with even the closest friends who have entered the ministry. A glass wall separates those of us in the secular world from them. They gesture, smile, bless, but they don't speak to us any longer. This, for example, seems to be a major reason why James Kavanaugh wrote *A Modern Priest Looks at His Outdated Church*. He wanted once again to need and be needed as a human being rather than to be regarded as some sort of sacred talisman. The gap of need is all important and it is a step backward in man's development for a *Deus ex*

---

[33] Bonhoeffer, *Letters and Papers* . . . . p. 165.
[34] *Ibid.*, p. 165.
[35] *Ibid.*, p. 120.

machina to fill it. An interesting and, I believe, clarifying parallel is provided by Buber's further explication of his I-Thou formula in which he refers to the "sphere of between" wherein a dialogue of response unfolds. The meaning of the formula, then, is in neither of the substantives but in the hyphen between. This gives us a new insight into responsibility; it is response to response; it is a convergence in which each finds his own reality, his Thou, in the other. After a particularly horrifying air raid Bonhoeffer noted "how we think at such times about those we should not like to live without, and forget all about ourselves. It makes one realize how closely our lives are bound up with other people's and in fact how our centre is outside of ourselves and how little we are individuals."[36] Perhaps the key sentence in *Letters and Papers from Prison* appears toward the end of the work: "God is the 'beyond' in the midst of our life."

The convergence resulting from an existential recognition of God's absence is not limited to the personal I-Thou relationship. Bonhoeffer sees the absence as a central fact of the secular world.

> There is no longer any need for God as a working hypothesis, whether in morals, politics or science. Nor is there any need for such a God in religion or philosophy. In the name of intellectual honesty these working hypotheses should be dropped or dispensed with as far as possible.[37]

Admittedly Bonhoeffer's position is paradoxical. At times he seems to be playing with words, if not ideas. "The God who is with us is the God who forsakes us (Mark 15:34). The God who makes us live in this world without using Him as a working hypothesis is the God before whom we are ever standing. Before God and with Him we live without God."[38] Such statements begin to make sense only when this absence of God is seen as divine play. Once again we have the emotional gap between separated friends. God has gradually absented Himself with felicity awhile that we may fulfill our-

36 *Ibid.*, p. 65.
37 *Ibid.*, p. 218.
38 *Ibid.*, p. 219.

selves by meeting Him in the "sphere of between." Since some of us at least have evolved beyond herd animals, we have no need for a good shepherd. It is God that now presents Himself as powerless in the world. "Matthew 8:17 makes it crystal clear that it is not by his omnipotence that Christ helps us, but by his weakness and suffering."[39]

Even as man realizes himself through unreserved entrance into the finite and the limited in his life and death, so the immanent God realizes Himself in the continuing event of the incarnation and crucifixion perpetuated in man. Such an "event" has connections everywhere. I think of Teilhard. For the Jesuit, the humanity of Christ embraces not only the human race but also the cosmos insofar as this is united to man, that is to say, insofar as evolution produces man, and insofar as man freely fosters that personal unity in the noosphere which is the key of evolutionary progress. For Teilhard there was a continuous creation as God exercised his creative power in and through Christ. What Bonhoeffer describes as "God allow[ing] himself to be edged out of the world and on the cross" is but the negative way of expressing Teilhard's view that the transcendence of God becomes of less importance in our thinking as Christ incorporates Himself in man's actions. The evolution Teilhard writes of is today a technological, computerized, electronic convergence which is also spiritual. Christ is involved in what the priest calls "creative union." It is an I-Thou convergence proceeding to the ultimate level, Omega. Such a view of "creative union" leads Teilhard to the same secular view as Bonhoeffer when he writes in *The Phenomenon of Man:* "Charity no longer demands that we merely bind up wounds; it urges us to build a better world here on earth and to be in the first ranks of every campaign for the full development of mankind."[40]

Bonhoeffer's ultimate vision of God may actually be similar to Teilhard's. It is not necessary for me to comment further

[39] *Ibid.*, p. 220.
[40] Teilhard de Chardin, *op. cit.*, p. 304.

on Teilhard's fundamental belief in the emergence of a noosphere formed of the radial energy of man's will and intellect. There are indications that Bonhoeffer was approaching a similar position. In one of his letters he quotes a section of Ecclesiastes which includes the statement "and God seeketh again that which is passed away." Bonhoeffer understands this to mean "that God gathers up again with us our past, which belongs to us." Thus "we can always remind ourselves that that is but one of the many hours that God is holding ready for us. . . . It means that nothing is lost, everything is taken up again in Christ, though of course it is transfigured in the process, becoming transparent, clear and free from all self-seeking and desire."[41] This parallels Teilhard's view right down to the transformation of matter, matter "without the distortion which results from human sin" (Bonhoeffer). Later Bonhoeffer meditates on the words the poet Paul Gerhardt has his Christ-child speak: "*Ich bringe alles wieder*," and applies them to those who ask about their relation to their dead. " 'I bring all again' that is we cannot and ought not to take them for ourselves, but allow Christ to give them back to us."[42]

These three answers to the questions of Church, Secularity and God are, of course, tentative. Bonhoeffer was in the process of working them out when his life was cut short at the age of thirty-nine. Of the *Letters and Papers*, which itself is not overly long and totally unsystematic, only about eighty pages are of theological significance. But these probes nevertheless caught the interest of laymen and theologians. He caught the mood of the times in his rejection of the closed morality of traditional Christianity which refused to accept man's evolution into adulthood. The staggering courage of his conviction is equalled only by Teilhard, who also projected his theory of man coming into his adult inheritance at a time when the world was torn apart with the bestial actions of childishly irresponsible men. Teilhard, I think, would agree

---

[41] Bonhoeffer, *Letters and Papers* . . . , p. 114.
[42] *Ibid.*, p. 114.

with Bonhoeffer's spirited defense of the adulthood of the
world against the attack by Christian apologetics:

> The attack . . . I consider to be in the first place pointless,
> in the second ignoble, and in the third un-Christian. Pointless,
> because it looks to me like an attempt to put a grown-up man
> back into adolescence, i.e., to make him dependent on things
> on which he is not in fact dependent any more, thrusting him
> back into the midst of problems which are in fact not prob-
> lems for him any more. Ignoble, because this amounts to an
> effort to exploit the weakness of man for purposes alien to him
> and not freely subscribed to by him. Un-Christian, because for
> Christ himself is being substituted one particular stage in the
> religiousness of man.[43]

As Auden has it in the passage from *For The Time Being*
which I quoted earlier in this chapter, we are in a world
where "There are bills to be paid, machines to keep in
repair,/ Irregular verbs to learn." We must redeem the time,
turning fate into providence by turning "its" into "thous."
For the present, being a Christian or a Jew or an atheist is
not trying to be different from other men. It is trying to be
yourself, trying to do your own thing, trying to find out who
you are in your encounters with others. As for God, God *is*,
and His "is" is manifest in man's functioning. As Martin Buber
once observed, in the day of judgment the Lord would not
ask him "Why were you not like Moses or Elijah?" but "Why
were you not like Martin Buber?" The last judgment is going
on in the instant we call our lives, and it is in our confrontation with the world of bills, machines and verbs that the
miracle can happen of man being God and God being man.

Buber and Bonhoeffer are not only spokesmen for new and
converging religions, but symbolic in their lives of the message they articulate. In turning, now, to Roman Catholicism
there probably is no figure more symbolic of convergence
than Pope John XXIII. He became a living example of the
religious leader who thought about and felt for all men, not
just his own flock. He was one who knew that Catholicism
had to involve itself once again with the secular world, that

---

[43] *Ibid.*, pp. 196–197.

there had to be a reconceptualizing of the Church's dogma, that an effort had to be made to find the truths shared by men of good faith. But John was the forerunner, the initiator, the catalyst, rather than the formulator of new approaches. His opening address to Vatican II was the initial signpost on a road others are now taking. In that speech he encouraged the council to adopt a historical and secular perspective: to "look to the present, to new conditions and new forms of life . . . to dedicate ourselves with an earnest will and without fear to that work which our era demands of us." Thus, though I do not consistantly refer to him, John XXIII's vision is, I hope, reflected in the foregoing chapters, and is, I believe, reflected in this chapter which, ending with observations on *The Future of Belief* (1966) by the Catholic theologian, Leslie Dewart, brings together Jew, Protestant and Catholic. It is a radical vision which permits the contacting — if not yet the converging — of Protestants and Catholics, Christians and Jews. More than that, it is a vision which permits a relationship between atheist and believer in a common recognition of brotherhood.

Dewart is not a modern legend as are Buber, Bonhoeffer and John XXIII, nor is there likelihood of his becoming one. His thought is compressed, his style uninviting; his appeal seems to be largely to other theologians. But *The Future of Belief* has sold well and has provoked much discussion in Protestant and Catholic groups. Apparently readers find behind the forbidding theological jargon, a real human being coming to grips with issues about which they are genuinely concerned. He is extending the views of thinkers such as Bonhoeffer directly into the reconsiderations occasioned by Vatican II, and he is doing it with a true revolutionary spirit.

He is not afraid of revolution. A child in Spain at a time when that country was torn apart by revolution, a bomber pilot in World War II, and a defender of Castro's revolution in the world press, Dewart is very much the secularly committed man for whom theology is not an academic discipline but a search for meaning, for truth, and for God. And he is willing to search in the most secular quarters to enrich his insights. In his book he relies not only on Bonhoeffer and Teilhard, but on Marx and Freud. If these four have nothing else in common, they at least are all revolutionaries, but in reading Dewart we discover that they all have surprising affinities, indeed provide logical lines of convergence.

Dewart is perhaps the most unorthodox of modern Catholic theologians, and yet his thoughts converge not only with contemporary thinkers but with Victorians as well, which indicates how long the problem of the Church and the secular world has been with us. One hundred years ago, in 1868, Matthew Arnold warned in "Hebraism and Hellenism" that the only way Christianity could survive in the modern world was through secularizing of its dogmas; i.e., a movement away from fundamentalism toward symbolic interpretation. As Arnold saw the Anglo-Catholic institution, there was in it altogether too much Hebraism — which he identified with closed morality — and not enough of the Hellenic — which he identified with open morality. Dewart shifts the labels but he holds similar views. For him Christianity's most serious problem in working out an integration with the everyday experience of contemporary man rests in an Hellenic rigidity which he calls conformity. This conformity is evidenced in the standard view of dogma as static and deity as transcendent. However, the inverse parallel to Arnold does not follow. Dewart does not see the answer in Hebraism (though I hope to point out a fundamental I-Thou tenet in Dewart's theories) but in a reconceptualization of the Church's role in the world, as well as of the notion of God and of the truth of dogma, a reconceptualization that has been referred to by Louis Dupré in *Commonweal* (February 10, 1967) as "symbolization."

The reconceptualization of dogma recalls another Victorian. John Henry Newman's *Essay on The Development of Christian Doctrine* is cited by Dewart as one of the modern evidences that Catholicism has been moving away from its stagnant position and gradually accepting the premise "that

Christian dogma must be said *in some real sense* to develop and, indeed, to have been developing since earliest times." At least from the time of Newman there has been a recognition that revelation was like a seed which could germinate and develop as a maturing plant with the developing and maturing needs of man. Dewart emphasizes the need for general acceptance and understanding of this insight. He warns that the Hellenic and static view of dogma goes hand in hand with the Hellenic and static view of man whose protean, evolving being is reduced to a procrustean conformity. Dogma as ungerminated seed had its place in Christianity's seed time, but we have moved toward harvest. There has been an evolution of man's mind through an infolding of knowledge and part of that knowledge is Christian dogma. To refuse to admit that evolution is to deny Christian dogma its place in the secular sun, is to let the truth become deformed in the shadows of restrictive ignorance.

Evolution in dogma and in man brings us to Dewart's acknowledged debt to the philosophy of Teilhard. He writes of Teilhard's profoundly positive view that "when coupled with the discovery of cosmic evolution, the experience of the spatio-temporal vastness of the universe reveals the new unsuspected dimension along which man's relation to reality should be measured."[44] As with Teilhard, Dewart sees this dimension to be an infolding of man's intellect, a growing awareness through which "we become conscious of that . . . we already were conscious of." Applying this specifically to doctrinal development, Dewart emphasizes that:

> we can begin to understand not only that, in fact, Christianity develops, but also the reason why it develops and the anthropological mechanism of its development. The understanding of man's psychic life in terms of consciousness, rather than knowledge, creates the possibility of understanding the truth of the Christian faith in such a way as would not only permit true development to occur, but indeed as requiring it by its very nature as truth. For . . . truth need no longer be understood as an essentially constant, and substantially immutable, though

[44] Leslie Dewart, *The Future of Belief* (New York: Herder & Herder, 1967), p. 24.

accidentally variable, relation to an immutable object objectively presented to the Christian intellect.[45]

His position on the mutual evolution of the thing being observed (dogma in this case) and the observer is arresting. He holds that man's consciousness is the matrix to which everything is connected and in which everything takes shape. As this consciousness grows, the connections to the other factors in the event are altered — that is to say truth is relative; it is a relational matter, and the relationship is once again I-Thou. It is a form of relativity that G. M. Hopkins dealt with in his theory of instress/inscape; it is a relativity that Dewart attributes to John XXIII who, he believes, was inspired by the insight

> that the truth of Christianity needs for its health, protection and development the reality of man's individual and cultural growth in self-consciousness. Despite hesitations and misgivings that have abounded as the implications of this act of faith have come to light, this remains for the present the Church's most fundamental principle of self-guidance — and, as we all sense, one which could not now be foresworn without the certainty of disaster.[46]

I am not playing with terms when I juxtapose and practically equate relativity and relationship as understood in Dewart. To Dewart "a concept is true if it causes . . . a true human experience as such (that is, as conscious)." He holds that every concept must in some way be true but that "it would be better to say that the concept is true to the *degree* that by its elevation of experience to consciousness it permits the truth of human experience to come into being." Thus the arrival at a further state of truth is an evolution produced through the encounter with another who forces us to modify our own position on a concept. There is a passage from Hegel that has been echoing in my mind during the writing of this chapter which nicely sums up Dewart's position. Paraphrasing its thrust, I can put it as follows:

---

[45] *Ibid.*, p. 84.
[46] *Ibid.*, pp. 172–173.

In proportion as we love truth, we shall be anxious to know what it is that leads our opponents to believe as they do. We shall begin to suspect that the pertinacity of belief exhibited by them arises from the perception of some aspect of truth which we have not perceived and we shall attempt to supplement that portion of the truth discovered by us with the portion discovered by them.

However, the encounter is more personal than Hegel would have us believe, more personal and more complex. To clarify his position Dewart quotes Karl Rahner on the experience of love. Dewart explains that for his purposes, if we substitute the word "consciousness" for "love" we have an apt analogy for his own position on the evolution of truth.

> The lover knows of his love: this knowledge of himself forms an essential element in the very love itself. The knowledge is infinitely richer, simpler and denser than any body of propositions about the love could be. Yet this knowledge never lacks a certain measure of reflexive articulateness: the lover confesses his love at least to himself, 'states' at least to himself something about his love. . . . In this progressive self-achievement, in which love comprehends itself more and more, in which it goes on to state something "about" itself and comprehends its own nature more clearly, the love itself becomes ordered; it has an increasing understanding of what must properly be the foundation of its own activity, mirrors its own nature with increasing clarity, approaches as its goal, with an increasingly clear awareness, what it always has been.[47]

I would have you note how strikingly similar the Dewart-Rahner position is to that of Buber. We have the encounter transforming an impersonal "It" into a "Thou." The Thou of the encounter mirrors our own Thou back to us, thus achieving that which "always has been," the ground of being, the "beyond in our midst." Such consciousness includes science, includes atheism, includes all forms of religion, for it can transcend concepts. Thus Dewart ends this demanding section of his work with the conclusion that "the traditional Christian faith can be cast not only in the traditional concepts but also in the novel emergent concepts that an evolving human experience creates."

---

[47] Dewart, op. cit., p. 117.

With such a position, convergence is possible on all levels. Dewart draws from Freud and from atheistic Marxism to confirm or reconceptualize his views of Christianity. Both approaches put the emphasis upon man's own actions. Freud in his *The Future of an Illusion* warns that modern man "will have to confess that he is no longer the centre of creation, no longer the object of the tender care of a benevolent providence. . . . Man cannot remain a child forever; he must venture at last into the hostile world."[48] Both Dewart and Bonhoeffer would agree with this position. Indeed Dewart even uses Freud's title as the basis for the title of his own work. However Freud's position varies from theirs profoundly. Freud saw faith as a prop for man in his prescientific ignorance, but now, though man is essentially the same weak creature, he must put away the things of a child. Freud held a dogmatic, static attitude toward the psychology of human development and did not even speculate about the development of dogma. Recall Norman O. Brown's telling attack upon Freud's static and pessimistic psychology. When compared to Teilhard's scientific humanism, Freud's position seems insufficiently humanistic. Teilhard was able to see all man's meaningful activities in the context of a cosmic evolution which permitted an ever-emerging awareness and ever-increasing emphasis upon man's will. This development was not grounds for a repudiation of faith, but for an affirmation of a faith that had developed along with man's ability to be conscious of the implications of that faith.

For Dewart, the modern Marxist position is best represented by Roger Garaudy, whose atheism springs from a profound belief in man and only secondarily from a denial of God's existence. Such atheism is, according to Dewart, relative and conditional: "It is conditioned by its prior commitment to man, and it is relative to a concept of God according to which he is existentially incompatible with man." That modern Christianity must make a "commitment to man" is the main tenet of the "secular city" theology. It is, then, only

---

[48] *Ibid.*, p. 86.

the concept of God that sets Marxism and Christianity at odds. Dewart denies even suggesting "that Marxism is a crypto-theism or a theism of intention." However, he does feel that the major immediate goal of each is the same and that the I-Thou relationship that could take place in a dialogue between the two would be rewarding to both. Here is where the reconceptualization of God would be of tremendous importance. By freeing ourselves of the moralistic deity "up there" and emphasizing the God "in here" we might be able to see that even the God that is absent for the Marxist is but another aspect of God. Even "St. John of the Cross," writes Dewart, "did not hesitate to refer to his own 'experience of the absence of God.' . . . In finding either the absence or the presence of God we have to do with a fundamental mode of self-and-world consciousness which is concretized in a radical resolve, that is, in a commitment of oneself, to a certain *projected* existence."[49] The orthodox Christian acts as though God were totally transcendent; the Marxist acts as though God were totally immanent. Today the gap in their encounter is not in their shared objective to ease suffering and promote human evolution but in a concept. In the attempt to fill that gap, not with the word or concept of God, but with understanding, both sides have much to learn. Little wonder that Bonhoeffer could feel more comfortable in talking about God to nonbelievers than to believers.

Whether modern humanism manifests itself through Freudianism, Marxism, Christianity or some form of convergence of these, Dewart readily admits the Pelagian implications. If we "emphasize the utter reality and puissance of man's freedom" he writes in *Commonweal* (Feb. 10, 1967) and de-emphasize God's providence, "this doctrine, not illogically issues in the conclusions of Pelagius." For fear of such heresy "Christianity's sense of God's immanence became dulled" and consequently "the Christian God became increasingly unbelievable. For at the limiting case, a strictly transcendent God is both utterly unreasonable and thoroughly

---

[49] *Ibid.*, pp. 58–59.

immoral; whereas, at the other extreme, a strictly immanent God may amount to no Christian God at all, but is not positively absurd and is at least superficially moral."[50] And Dewart seems to be in the main current of progressive thinking in the Church in making this point. A New Catechism (1967), an American translation of the new Dutch Catechism holds that it is "necessary to view God . . . free of the world, but . . . still at the depth of its being [the beyond in our midst]. God is independent of man, but He is still bound up with man. . . . Hence we may still see in post-Christian religions and ideologies such as Islam, Humanism and Marxism an unconscious longing and a roundabout search for the true image of Christ which we Christians so often obscure."[51]

The implications of this new catechism in relation to Dewart's thinking about reconceptualizing Christianity are far-reaching. When one compares this catechism's open, discursive and secularly oriented treatment of theological questions to the closed, definitive and other-worldly answers of the Baltimore Catechism, Number 2, answers that are still seared into the memory of many a Catholic who had to parrot them back before receiving First Holy Communion, the contrast says it all. But it is not enough. This new catechism which attempts to use language intelligible to modern man still does not reconceptualize; however, the modern language and conversational approach may lead to reconceptualization. A catechism in itself is anathema to Dewart. For him "the establishment of man's relation of truth to reality can only be an intensification of the reality that man already has. It follows from this that the nature of truth does not merely permit truth to develop, but indeed requires that it do so."[52] Truth — and by extension, Christianity — rests not with one formulation nor is encompassed by one man's belief. It is a cultural entity rather like an amoeba which, feeding on its environment and having its principle of life within it, con-

---

[50] Dewart, "God and the Supernatural," Commonweal, February 10, 1967, p. 526.

[51] A New Catechism (New York: Herder and Herder, 1967), p. 58.

[52] Dewart, The Future of Belief, pp. 110–111.

stantly changes its shape in its encounters with the consciousness of man. Obviously such a view of the developing Church can be paralleled to Teilhard's converging noosphere, to Fuller's continuous man, even in a lesser degree to McLuhan's global tribe. As Dewart himself observes:

> Man's ultimate achievement is not found in the circumscription of his personality. It is found on the contrary in its communication and expansion beyond itself into another self, indeed, into a community of selves. The ultimate hope of Christian faith is not that man should achieve *within himself* the act of beholding God, a vision close enough to constitute an intimate union with God; it is to achieve an intimate union with every person through a union with God *in God himself.*[53]

Dewart's book is an effort to bridge Teilhard's speculative vision with Bonhoeffer's practical concerns through reconceptualizing the notion of God. I am intrigued with the work not because I am satisfied with his conclusions but because in the effort he sees the need to draw from every contemporary source, a need representative of the mood of convergence that typifies the most exciting thinkers of our time. Whether it be Teilhard, Fuller, Watts or the hippies, the effort is the same, to realize the God within not through definition but through the fully realized life. Dewart's conclusions on how to conceive of God are baffling. He holds that "God is not a Being," "God cannot be said to exist," and "God has no essence" — although, I admit that with this last negation, he does add that God must "be thought of as having essence," so as not to leave the mind without any object. The speculations that explore these propositions are difficult to follow, let alone summarize, but it is clear that Dewart is anxious to free us from as many concrete and smug assumptions about God as possible. As with Buber and Bonhoeffer, he is radical if not revolutionary in his insistence on fidelity rather than conformity and his vision is directed, as with all the thinkers dealt with in this book, to the future.

---

[53] *Ibid.,* p. 188.

Voices of Dissent:
A Conclusion

Looking back on the chapters of this book and their headings, I feel uneasy. It must seem willfully bizarre of me to juxtapose such dissimilar figures as the Jesuit paleontologist, Teilhard, with the dramatist, Shaw, or the rabbi, Martin Buber; theologians and psychologists with the hippies; the secular city of Harvey Cox with the futuristic vision of Buckminster Fuller; the electronic probes of Marshall McLuhan with diffuse generalities about modern aesthetics. My excuse may seem equally bizarre: I claim that I am not competent to deal with any of these juxtapositions in an authoritative way. I am thus rescued from pretentiousness. What is offered here is not the result of intensive research, but the shadow of things to come caught in a kind of peripheral vision while I have been focusing on other work. I most certainly am not dismissing "the voices of convergence," but I am admitting that the logical lines holding the various chapters together probably do not always seem inevitable, perhaps not even logical, to all readers. On the other hand, I hope that the cumulative impact of the parallels, echoes and similarities herein suggested may encourage some to see the same wide, interlinking pattern I think realizable if we but seize the dream and apply our wills and intellects.

I have absorbed enough McLuhan to distrust the expert in any given field. The scholar in any of the fields so cavalierly glossed over in this book is bound to use terms in describing it such as "superficial," "hasty," "inadequate." I would like to persuade him to see this book in another light. Perhaps it can be seen as a sort of creative disorder in which clear lines of demarcation converge into mutually supporting meaning. The sacred and the secular have converged; science and religion have converged; within science, physics and biology seem to be breaking down their usual barriers; within re-

gions, Protestant and Catholic, Christian and Jew, believer
nd atheist, seem to carry on meaningful dialogue. The im-
ortant work is being done in middle areas, fields such as
iochemistry, molecular biology, physical chemistry. Yeats
ight say that "mere anarchy is loosed" but it is not enough;
is another type of order we have here in this age of the
lectronic "second coming," one in which it is necessary to
e a number of facets simultaneously before grasping the
omplex event. I touched on modern art in the third chapter,
ut aside from the prefatory poems and passages for each
hapter, I have avoided literature. G. B. Shaw, I saw as a
heological philosopher. In terms of McLuhan's theory, I
elt I was seriously and dangerously competent in the literary
rea. I was "hot." I would not have been able to juggle my
terary insights with the same casualness. I would not have
een able to maintain the fruitful creative disorder of the
iddle area.

It also seems in retrospect that I have been juxtaposing
wo or three facets of my own personality. I made no attempt
o assume a consistent and particular *persona*. Certainly I
ad no intention of taking the "true believer" stance replete
ith evangelical enthusiasm. I simply wanted to share the
atisfaction of a pattern I had caught in the midst of seeming
ontradictions. I limited myself to the one or two most readily
vailable works of the authors cited and thus hoped that the
eader would refer to the sources himself if he found these
xploratory essays interesting. I realize, too, that the tone of
hese chapters varies. Some of them are a great deal more
ersonal than others. The wide spectrum of material dictated
his shifting. When writing about an LSD experience one
ust, of course, be more impressionistic than when grappling
ith Teilhard's theory of the noosphere. Again my reserva-
ons about Harvey Cox or Marshall McLuhan seem all the
ore conservative in relation to my open admiration for
uller or Bonhoeffer. But these contradictions are more
pparent than real. It would be a falsification of my ex-
erience of these various thinkers to level them all to a

similar approach and tone. The convergence of insights i
faith, science, economics, aesthetics, architecture, politic:
all had different impacts on me, though the total effect w;
and is a positive one.

However wide the range of thinkers and however uneve
the tone, I believe the overall effect is essentially a unifie
one. I make continuing references to preceding chapter:
suggesting, for example, how far McLuhan could be dealt wit
in the context of Fuller's thinking, how Brown can also b
seen in relation to scientific theorists, how the hippies ca
be seen as part of the new secular Christianity adumbrate
by Bonhoeffer and enunciated by Dewart. The effect I hope
for was a sense of total convergence in which all the chaptei
could be seen as but one simultaneous event held in a unifie
impression in the reader's mind.

Convergence in the sense I use it in this book first becam
evident to me in my reading of Teilhard. In the final analysi
whatever unity this series of essays has, whatever truth it r
flects, derives from the writings of Teilhard de Chardin. Th
influence of his thinking is every bit as basic in the las
chapter where his name is only mentioned in passing as i
the first chapter in which I outline the whole cosmic coi
vergence vision in terms of his *The Phenomenon of Man*.
deliberately faced the possibilities of heresy in his work in th
beginning so that in the final chapter on the new secula
Church, I could suggest that the whole evolutionary concep
even granting its pantheistic, Pelagian and Manichaean tenc
encies was not revolutionary and unorthodox at all but
radical increase in awareness which could be read as an evolu
tion of dogma itself.

For me, at least, my renewed interest and increasing excite
ment in Catholicism is directly attributable to the Church'
return to the concerns of this world. Teilhard's emphasi
upon earthly evolution leading to cosmic evolution and ult
mately to an incorporation with the divine Evolutor Himseli
Christ, prepared the way for that secular return. The "voice
of convergence" that I have singled out in the course of th;

ook, whether they are aware of Teilhard or not, are con-
ibuting to that religious evolution, and in that sense they
n be seen as secular saints. I'm certainly not recommending
at you should invoke Saint Buckminster Fuller, Saint David
izelon etc. but that, if you have faith in the secular church,
u should read them.

I am aware, too, how much that I have written about the
ossibilities of fruitful convergence must seem to many like
much whistling in the dark. I wrote on the hippie move-
ent in July, 1967. By November of the same year, the hip-
es were reported dead as a significant influence, and it was
ear that the press, if not the public, had lost interest in their
ternative to the greed-fear society. However, in writing
out them a few months ago or in writing about them now,
made and make no claim that they or any other group or
rsons have total solutions for contemporary problems. It
enough that they made the attempt to drop out and in the
ocess caught the imagination of many in their generation
d a number in my generation. In part they were cynically
ploited by the press and the entertainment world whose
g business advertisers have for their own good reasons — or
ot so good reasons — become disturbed; in part, they were
ctims of organized crime, always so much more carefully
otected than idealists in our society; in part, they were vic-
ns of their own excesses; but in toto, they still seem to me
rows pointing the way. When their enthusiasm can converge
ith those leaders such as Martin Buber who offer the possi-
lities of communes in a larger society that would use its
sources to protect rather than destroy, their dream can be
alized.

The fluctuations in the fortunes of the hippies are symp-
matic of the much more serious problem of entropy — not
nysical energy dispersal, but deep-rooted conservatism. There
e voices of dissent in our time that can not only slow down
e anticipated merging but perhaps halt and reverse trends
at have begun. There was no theologian in my youth whom
more admired than Jacques Maritain, yet his recent highly

conservative attack upon what he called "Teilhardism" seen
to me to reveal more than just a rigid stand on doctrine.
is a rigid stand against secularity generally. I know too that
is upon Teilhardism that my faith and the faith of at lea
half a dozen of my acquaintances stands. I do not delude m
self with the comfortable thought that the eighty-five-ye:
old Maritain is senile and represents an uninfluential po•
tion. On the contrary. His mind is clear, his style is
felicitous as ever, and his position very much a part of tl
present-day Church. Newman's views one hundred years a;
on the development of dogma were condemned as "moder
ism." Teilhard's views are coming under the same attacks a•
same labeling today. Maritain represents a strong and vo•
faction — perhaps majority — in the church hierarchy wh•
he writes of Teilhard in U. S. Catholic (November, 196•
that "it was nothing for Marx and Engels to turn Hegel u•
side down, but to turn Christianity upside down, so that it
no longer rooted in the Trinity and the Redemption but
the evolving Cosmos is quite a different matter." Marita•
holds that Vatican II gave no encouragement to the mov•
ment which he ironically refers to as "better Christianity•
And continuing his irony he suggests that "the partisans •
Teilhardism . . . will have to wait for a new Council, a•
another, and Lord knows how many after that. Or else,
their patience wears thin, will they go so far as to for•
themselves into a separate sect?" It's the old conservati•
heresy-sniffing again. Faced with a return to such cons•
vatism, I suspect Christ Himself would once again becom•
a social dropout and join the Essenes, or the Hasidic co•
mune, or the Catholic Worker Farm, or become a hippi•
or whatever group was available that would offer him t•
opportunity of thinking out ways of "redeeming the tim•
from insignificance."

Maritain, in dismissing Teilhard's theories of ultima•
convergence, refers to them as "theology-fiction" and "fra•
ments of a vast poem." In my undergraduate days I rememb•
Maritain's Creative Intuition in Art and Poetry, which i•

fluenced me profoundly. I wonder if Maritain still subscribes
to its tenets. When he sees Teilhard's creative intuition, his
"invisible flame," as a weakness in the theologian, I think he
is exposing instead the weakness of traditional dogma which
can no longer accept intuition and inspiration as part of its
own development. Newman refers to the "illative sense"
which permits us to confirm our faith simultaneously through
intellect, imagination, memory, sense, through, in a word,
the entire man. That was what Maritain saw as creative intuition in the field of aesthetics. Because a religious theory
has begun with such a unified insight does not degrade it;
rather it elevates it. Whatever one calls it: event, prehensive
unity, convergence, illative sense, it all comes down to a
refusal to see the sources of knowledge as separated; it refuses
to see man, God and evolution as separated.

I have prefaced the chapters of this book with poems and
literary passages as well as consistently made references in
the text to Blake, Yeats, Eliot, Hopkins, Arnold and the
Romantic poets. In every case the reference was made to
underscore the convergence of creative intuitions in literature and the insights and theories of thinkers in practical
and speculative fields. That Teilhard's theories as described
by Maritain are the result "of a quite peculiar kind of spiritual
experience" reinforced "with great scientific dreams" does
in no way suggest weakness. For me, at least, Maritain is describing a man who as priest and poet and scientist was a
living example of the fruitful convergence taking place in
our time.